"This book is an excellent retirement planning guide with a special emphasis on Social Security planning and benefits. Since many Americans will spend as much or more time in retirement than they did working, this book may prove to be your best lifetime investment!"

—*Sean A. McGee CFA, CFP, wealth management advisor,*
*from a major global investment firm,*
*Bridgewater, New Jersey*

"What is clear from reading this book is that when to start collecting Social Security is anything but the automatic decision most people assume it to be. You should decide when to begin receiving payments based on the factors Steve discusses, not the number of birthdays you have celebrated."

—*Timothy L. Krongard,*
*venture capital firm, CFO,*
*QuestMark Partners, Baltimore, Maryland*

"This is a fascinating book. In my opinion, the book is quite comprehensive and addresses a number of issues. The key points regarding the decision to take Social Security benefits early is particularly helpful and probably not well understood by many recipients. I also found the sections addressing appropriate withdrawal rates for portfolios to be quite comprehensive and helpful."

—*Larry Puglia, mutual fund portfolio manager,*
*billions under his management,*
*Baltimore, Maryland*

"Like many baby boomers, I thought an early retirement and a part-time job would be the ideal way to get out of the rat race. After reading this book, I realized that my plan was flawed. What an eye-opening journey into the real costs of early retirement!"

—*Helen Gioulis (still planning an early retirement,*
*but hasn't yet figured how), catalog manager,*
*Philadelphia, Pennsylvania*

"During my career on the financial side of the oil and gas business, I continually concentrated on maximizing my savings. As I neared retirement, I had not considered all the planning issues that Steve has identified. Using the steps described in the book, you are sure to avoid a $100,000 mistake in your retirement planning."

—*Charles F. Cadenhead (retired early),*
*finance director, Chevron Texaco,*
*Houston, Texas*

"Any Baby Boomer should have this book and really read this! It is exceedingly good. I learned a lot and decided correctly to wait!"

—*Jim Miller (planned an early retirement,*
*but decided to delay retirement),*
*industrial sales representative,*
*Philadelphia, Pennsylvania*

"A must-have retirement planning book. I have always been told by my parents to contribute to my 401(k) and everything would be fine. Well, this book teaches you that it takes more than that to retire early or otherwise. You must get this book for yourself and your family and put it into practice."

—*Lee Anne Beard (wants to retire early),*
*program planner, The Home Shopping Network,*
*St. Petersburg, Florida*

"Silbiger makes a complex process simple and easy to understand All workers from executives to new hires can benefit by gaining better understanding of what their Social Security options are an his book serves as an excellent guide."

—*Michael V. Jamison (advises clients about retiremer*
*commercial banker, Wachovia Ba*
*Philadelphia, Pennsylva*

RETIRE
EARLY?
MAKE THE
SMART
CHOICES

**Also by Steven Silbiger:**

*The Ten-Day MBA*

# RETIRE EARLY?

## MAKE THE SMART CHOICES

**STEVEN A. SILBIGER, CPA**

 Collins

*An Imprint of* HarperCollins*Publishers*

This book is designed to provide information on the subject of Social Security benefits and retirement planning. Some of the material in the book concerns laws that are changed periodically and therefore the readers need to seek the most recent updates for decision making. Neither the author nor the publisher is engaged in rendering legal, accounting, or other professional services by publishing this book. Particular questions arising from this book should be answered by the appropriate professional to ensure that they have been addressed appropriately. Nor do they assume liability for any loss, or risk which is incurred as a consequence, directly or indirectly, of the use and application of any of the contents of this work, and any such liability is hereby expressly disclaimed.

HarperCollins books may be purchased for educational, business, or sales promotional use. For information please write: Special Markets Department, HarperCollins Publishers, 10 East 53rd Street, New York, NY 10022.

FIRST EDITION

Designed by Joy O'Meara

Library of Congress Cataloging-in-Publication Data

Silbiger, Steven.
    Retire early? make the smart choices / Steven Silbiger.—1st ed.
        p.    cm.
    ISBN-10: 0-06-079866-1
    ISBN-13: 978-0-06-079866-6
        1. Early retirement—United States—Planning.    2. Social Security—United States.    I. Title.

HD7110.5.U6S55    2005
332.024'014'0973—dc22                                           2005045952

05    06    07    08    09    DIX/RRD    10    9    8    7    6    5    4    3    2    1

# CONTENTS

# ACKNOWLEDGMENTS

I would like to thank my senior editor Herb Schaffner at HarperCollins for all his help and support. I would like to thank my personal editor Helen Gioulis for her diligent efforts to transform my drafts into this book. I also I would like to thank my agent Rafe Sagalyn of the Sagalyn Agency for his extraordinary ability to see my book's potential and quickly finding a good home for it at HarperCollins with my first book, *The Ten-Day MBA*.

Questions, comments? E-mail the author at
Retire.Early.Question@juno.com or visit our Web site at
*www.Retire-Early-Question.com*

# INTRODUCTION

### Social Security Administration Web site
*"Choosing when to retire is one of the most important decisions you will make in your lifetime."*

### The Wall Street Journal, 9/12/04
*"When you retire, what's your most critical financial decision? Deciding when to claim Social Security retirement benefits has got to be near the top of the list. (After all, for folks age 65 and up, Social Security accounts for 39% of income, far more than any other source.) Yet the media, investment advisors and academics spend precious little time discussing the ins and outs of Social Security, so it's hard for seniors to make an informed decision."*

### The Complete Idiot's Guide to Social Security
*"Decisions you make at retirement can impact your life for 20 to 30 years or more, depending on how long you live in retirement. Don't make the decisions lightly or on the spur of the moment."*

### Money magazine, 12/3/04
*"When to take Social Security? It's arguably the most important question retirees face."*

Self-help books have tackled most of the important questions in people's lives: which college to attend, how to choose a mate, what to name the baby. Shelves are filled with books by financial gurus about how to invest in stocks, mutual funds, and real estate, and how to avoid the taxman. But when you get near retirement age, the question is, "Should I retire early and take that early retirement check from Social Security?" Although it sounds like such a simple question, there is no simple answer, and the experts have surprisingly missed this big question.

When I couldn't find a book or even a good article on this subject, I decided to use my skills and experience to research and solve the Social Security question for you. I worked as a CPA for a national public accounting firm and earned my MBA from a top business school. Currently I am successfully running my own product development business. In my first book, *The Ten-Day MBA*, I distilled the subjects taught at the nation's top business schools into a comprehensible guide that readers can easily use. I am happy to say that hundreds of thousands of readers in over a dozen countries have been productively using *The Ten-Day MBA*. In this book I will give you the tools that will let you make the best retirement decisions possible. I will walk you through a process of deciding what to do with your Social Security benefits and how to plan for your retirement. Incredibly, some of the authoritative advice from the "experts" is dead wrong, and it is costing Americans many millions of dollars a year.

In just a few years, the first of an estimated 77 million Baby Boomers will become eligible for benefits and will have to make that decision. A full 32 percent of the workforce has no retirement savings set aside and 80 percent have no private pension. About two thirds of retirees receive 50 percent of their income from Social Security. Today about 20 percent of Social Security recipients rely on their checks as their sole source of income. Taking the Social Security check early at age 62 versus age 65 currently costs recipients 24 percent of their monthly benefits and that penalty is going up to 30 percent. Unexpected taxes and additional penalties can literally take away the rest.

I asked my friends who are financial planners with presti-

# THE $100,000 QUESTION:
## AN ILLUSTRATIVE CASE

My research has galvanized my belief that even well-educated, financially-aware people are in the dark about their Social Security benefits and their early retirement. To illustrate the point let's look at Nancy Kessler's situation.

Nancy Kessler is an active 61-year-old woman who is on the verge of opting for early retirement benefits next year. We met for lunch. She works as a marketing manager, the same job that she has held for twenty-two years. Nancy is divorced, living alone, active socially, and she plays golf when she gets a chance. She has a financial manager who reviews her investments and financial plans annually. When I asked her what she planned for her Social Security benefits she said, "I would rather have it now, rather than later. A bird in the hand is worth two in the bush." I said that choice is the correct one for many people, but why don't we go over a few issues and see where you land. "What do you have to lose?" Using the 7 Key Issues methodology we explored Nancy's choice. Many of her benefit and tax calculations mentioned here are written about in more depth in the chapters that follow.

## Step One: Know What Your Benefits Are

First we reviewed her Social Security Benefits Statement. This statement is sent annually to all workers age 25 and older. Her statement said that based on her salary of $50,000 and her past working history, she was entitled to a monthly benefit of $964 ($11,568 a year) if she opted for early retirement at age 62. The average monthly payment was $950 including a 2.7 percent cost-of-living adjustment in 2005.

If Nancy waited until her NRA of 66, she would be entitled to $1,355 a month, $16,260 a year. That is called her Primary

gious national investment firms about early retirement planning, and surprisingly, they don't deal with the issue. They agree they are more focused on savings and investments because that is the way they earn their money. When I started to explain to them the issues involved, they were unaware of the complexities and encouraged me to write this book so that they could better serve their clients.

For some, the early bird does get the worm and the most Social Security benefits by opting to receive early benefits. For others, the patient tortoise wins the race with the greatest payout by waiting until full retirement. It's a $100,000 question. For a couple, it may be a $200,000 question.

A recent survey found that 54 percent of workers are not even aware that the NRA has been raised from 65 to 67. No, it's not the National Rifle Association. The *Normal Retirement Age* is the term used for the age at which you collect full retirement benefits. This confusion about the full retirement age is puzzling, as 72 percent of workers surveyed by the National Council on the Aging said that qualifying for Social Security was their most important reason for the timing of their retirement. FRA is another abbreviation, representing Full Retirement Age, with just the same meaning as NRA, and both are often used interchangeably. This book covers all such acronyms, jargon, and rules that may confuse you.

Although the Social Security Act was signed seventy years ago, in 1935, the early retirement choice began in 1956, when Congress felt that slightly younger wives of 62 should receive benefits at the same time as their 65-year-old husbands. In 1961 legislators erased the discriminatory part of the rule and let both men and women receive early, albeit reduced, benefits at age 62. The decision became much more complicated when in 1983 the full retirement age was gradually increased from age 65 to 67, and benefits also began to be taxed for "upper income" retirees who chose to continue to work. This courageous, bipartisan move led by President Ronald Reagan risking reelection was supposed to extend the solvency of Social Security by decades because it compensated for increased enrollments and increased benefits. In 1977 President Jimmy Carter and the Congress had also made some heroic changes. They increased the Social Security payroll tax (FICA) from 6.45 percent to 7.65 percent, made changes to the cost of living adjustment formulas, and gradually reduced benefits. Despite these moves for solvency, the situation continues to grow worse because no political courage on either side of the aisle has been mustered in the last twenty years. Therefore, it is reasonable that the solvency of the Social Security system enter into your decision to take benefits sooner rather than later.

*Retire Early? Make the SMART Choices* leads you to the right answer about early retirement benefits based on your personal and family history, work plans, financial goals, and personal risk thresholds. It will distill all the complicated rules, formulas, and jargon into an understandable road map. Thousands of dollars of benefits hang in the balance with this single decision, and for some it may make the difference between a happy retirement and a life of meager means. To make this decision about Social Security and your retirement portfolio without all the facts is foolhardy. To make this decision knowing all the facts and ramifications is very smart.

In this book I plan to use a few abbreviations and acronyms to make the book more readable and to prepare you for the language used by the Social Security Administration personnel financial planners and the informational materials that they may give you. For example, the SSA means the institution called the Social Security Administration and TIPS are Treasury Inflation Protected Securities.

## THE SEVEN KEY ISSUES

Here is a summary of the seven key issues that affect the decision to elect early retirement benefits. These key issues will be carefully examined and explained so you will be able to apply the facts to your own situation.

1. What are the benefits available and what is the penalty for early retirement? What is at risk if you make the wrong decision? Do you realize that 56 percent of new retirees are opting to be early birds and many could be making a mistake, and some of the tortoises are equally mistaken by waiting?
2. How's your health? How long do you expect to live? How well is your spouse? What are the key health risks and how do they affect you?
3. Are you married? Your decision greatly affects how much your spouse collects. Surprisingly, the early retirement penalty to the spouse could be 67 percent of the spouse's benefits!
4. Are you planning to continue to work while receiving benefits? Did you know that tax consequences could wipe out all of your benefits?
5. What are your cash needs for retirement? Will your benefits be extra spending money or a major lifeline?
6. What forecast do you have for your own investments? having extra money now more important to you more money later?
7. How concerned are you about the projected insolvency the Social Security system?

To see how the method works for real people read study that follows.

Insurance Amount or PIA. For waiting 4 years, that is an additional $391 a month or $4,692 a year for all her retirement years remaining no matter how long she lived. If Nancy wanted to wait further, she could get $1,881 a month at age 70, practically double the early retirement figure. Nancy said that she never knew she had that many options.

## Step Two: How's Your Health?

The gamble with taking early retirement is that if you die early, you get the most total benefits, so you win. Actually, you lose, but you take the most cash out of the system. On the other hand, if you live to be a Methuselah you will get much smaller monthly benefits over your long lifetime.

Nancy said that her health was not that good, but I was skeptical. She said that she had smoked decades ago. She said that she tried to watch what she ate, but sometimes she admits she was "naughty." Plump but by no means obese is how I would describe her. I looked at what she was having for lunch, a chicken salad platter and a Snapple. I asked if she knew that the chicken salad was made with full-fat mayonnaise so it contained the fat of a double cheeseburger, and that Snapple had the same sugar content as a candy bar. She sarcastically asked me if we are going to talk about her retirement or her eating habits. "Retirement today," I said.

I asked her about how her mom was, knowing that they were close. "Mable is doing well. She is 90. She smoked until recently, and has smoked for most of her life." "And your dad?" I asked. "He died when he was 83, of pancreatic cancer." I said that her genetics told me that she was going to live a good, long time. I checked what the Social Security Administration calls its Period Life Table. Like life insurance companies' actuarial tables, it gives you an indication of your life expectancy based on age and sex and thousands of people's actual experience. For

Nancy the table said that as a woman of 62, she has the same life expectancy of her dad who died at 83. She did not like hearing that, but she felt that she was in much better health than he was during his lifetime.

Considering her parent's longevity and her own good health, we can assume a long life expectancy for Nancy. I consulted a table of break-even ages from the Social Security Administration (SSA) and assumed no penalties for working during early retirement. Nancy would break even on her Social Security payout at 76 years of age. In other words, if she lived longer than 76, then her total Social Security payout would be greater if she retired later and waited for the larger check.

### Step Three: Are You Married?

Nancy has been divorced for several years and has no dependent children. Being married was a key variable in some people's choice, I added. Opting for early retirement can also cut your non-working spouse's benefit by over half. To that, Nancy hopefully asked if she opted for early retirement, could it possibly slash her ex's benefits. I said, "It won't; if that were possible so many people would do it, that the projected shortfall in the Social Security trust fund would be wiped away."

### Step Four: Are You Planning To Work And Receive Early Retirement Benefits?

Nancy's financial advisor suggested that she work during her early retirement to supplement her income. Since she wants to live comfortably and not dip too much into her nest egg early on, that sounded like a good idea. Maybe not full time, but she hoped to work at a level that would provide her $25,000 a year, half of her current income of $50,000. Unfortunately, for earned incomes over $12,000 in 2005 (indexed for inflation), benefits will be reduced by $1 for every $2 of earnings over the limit. The SSA calls this its Annual Earnings Test. Her early benefits of $11,568 a year therefore would be reduced by $6,500 to $5,068, or more than half, until she reaches her full retirement age of 66, her NRA. In the last partial calendar year from January up to but not including your birthday month, the government reduces benefits only $1 for every $3 over the over a higher limit of $31,800 in 2005 (indexed for inflation). For Nancy this is not an issue as she was born in February.

In addition, the IRS may tax the reduced Social Security. Benefits are taxed if you earn above certain levels based on a formula to arrive at a Base Amount. This Base Amount is one-half of the Social Security benefits paid to you plus all your other earnings. An IRS worksheet takes the income number from your tax return's Aggregate Gross Income figure and then adds your tax-exempt interest, just to add insult to injury! On the other hand, the SSA penalizes only "actively" earned income to figure its penalties, so that Nancy's investment and real estate income would not be included in the Earnings Test that reduced her benefits as outlined in the prior paragraph.

If the Base Amount exceeds $25,000 for a single person ($32,000 for a married couple) then Nancy is taxed by the IRS on 50 percent of the benefits received. In this case Nancy has $5,068 in benefits, $25,000 of regular earnings, $2,300 profit from renting out her duplex, and $8,600 from dividends and interest on her portfolio. Unfortunately, her Base Amount totals $38,434, which is higher than an extra-special IRS provision for "upper income" seniors. For "wealthy" seniors earning above $34,000 as a single person or $44,000 for couples, 85 percent of their benefits are taxed, not just 50 percent. Using a 15 percent marginal tax rate applied to 85 percent of her benefits, Nancy's remaining benefits of $5,068 are further reduced by a tax of $646 to $4,422.

In total, her $11,568 of possible benefits, that she was expecting as her early retirement reward, has withered by 62 percent to $4,422 after reductions and taxes! Even if she were able to invest the entire early Social Security checks in an aggressive investment herself, it would not compensate her for the reduction in benefits.

Another issue came up for Nancy's friend Betty, who had lost her health insurance when she retired early. Medicare starts at age 65, so Betty has been responsible for paying for her own policy for three years. Her monthly cost for health insurance as an individual policy holder with fewer benefits and a higher deductible runs her about $400 a month or $4,800 a year, an amount that has increased dramatically recently. Nancy realizes that she will have to find a part-time job with health benefits or her entire early Social Security check could be eaten up.

## Step Five: What Are Your Retirement Needs?

Nancy told me that her advisor said that that she would need approximately 70 percent of her pre-retirement income during retirement. Her advisor was a bit optimistic because it could be higher. I told her that one thing that is important to know is that Social Security benefits have no taxes taken out. That means that those checks of about $12,000 represent a salary check of about $16,000 before all the federal, state, and local the taxes are deducted. "Social Security put that way is a large income," she said. Her advisor said that her portfolio including her IRAs, 401(k) and home equity would support her needs if she earned a modest income on a part-time basis and stayed within a budget. Nancy considered herself a conservative spender, but then she wondered what type of lifestyle had her advisor envisioned for her. She enjoyed the freedom to join friends going out to eat, golf, enjoying shore events, and vacationing, all without a real concern about the cost. That was not something she wanted to compromise. "What good would retirement be if I can't do what I want to? Maybe I will wait to retire later."

Estimating your financial needs during retirement is among "the most fundamental of planning steps but only 42 percent of workers haven't even made the attempt," according to the Employee Benefit Research Institute.

## Step Six: What Plans Do You Have For Your Investments?

Nancy has a conservative portfolio of 50 percent in stocks funds, 40 percent bonds and 10 percent cash. Any extra cash that is not invested directly into her 401(k) from her check is invested in a money market fund earning 1.25 percent, as a rainy day fund. In other words, any extra money that she may get from her Social Security benefits will not be poised for high growth returns in the market or pyramided into a real estate fortune.

As for the majority of investors, the stock market meltdown of 2001 and 2002 wiped away most of her gains from the bull market run up from 1998 to 2000. Understandably, she felt her future gains were not so certain. And her house's value may fall if interest rates continued to climb. She was concerned that her portfolio may not be the size she needs to really support the lifestyle she wanted. Nancy said that she might want to wait and see how the market goes and rethink early retirement.

I told her that on her sixty-second birthday the Social Security Administration was not going to ask for her retirement decision, nor would the early retirement door close until her NRA at age 66. She could wait, and take early benefits at any time before her NRA, and receive reduced benefits adjusted for the months that she does choose to wait. Waiting actually would increase her check each month that she puts off receiving benefits. That was a shock. Nobody had explained to Nancy that it was not an all-or-nothing decision. She had heard her friends talking about how happy they were to get their first checks as soon as possible and they never considered waiting. "Maybe they needed to talk to you first, Steve?" Nancy said with a smile.

Over 49 percent of Americans begin collecting Social Security benefits at age 62, the earliest age at which benefits are available. An El Paso man just turning 62 sums up the philosophy, "I want to start enjoying life. It goes so fast. You never know how long you have to live. I want to enjoy life, take a vacation. It's what everyone wants."

### Step Seven: Concerned About The Health Of Social Security?

Nancy first approached the answer with little concern. Rightfully so, since she is only a year from early retirement and only six years away from her full retirement check. Experts project the Social Security Trust Fund will go bankrupt in 2042, way beyond the year that Nancy plans to be gracing the earth with her presence. Social Security's solvency does not seem to be an issue for her, but maybe for her granddaughter.

This is the short version of the process that *Retire Early?* will lead you through to get to your own answer. I deal with Nancy's benefit and tax calculations in more depth in the rest of the book so that you can see the math and you can apply her example to your situation. Because no two retirees have identical situations or objectives, each case must be evaluated individually. No single chapter in this book should be considered in a vacuum. The process is a little like putting together a puzzle with many parts. In Nancy's case her best financial decision is the opposite of what she first intended to do. Adding it all up, she would be getting approximately $18,000 of net early retirement benefits after taxes over four years in exchange for $100,000 of benefits if she lives to her dad's age, and $200,000 if she lives to at least her mom's. For Nancy it truly was a $100,000 question. As you saw in Nancy's example, the cost of health insurance during early retirement and Social Security penalties on earned income became deciding factors. In her particular circumstances it makes sense to wait, but for others "take it now" makes equally good sense. Only by following the same steps outlined in the book can you be sure.

This book will deal with these Social Security topics, as well as budgeting for retirement, investing during retirement, and other peripheral issues, such as consumer scams specifically targeting people near retirement that can be equally important. This book contains all the tools and resources that you will need to arrive at an intelligent and thoughtful decision. I provide worksheets for your own calculations. I also lead you through the Social Security application process in chapter 10 and provide follow-up resources in chapter 14. Millions of people will face their $100,000 early retirement decision and need help. So let's begin the process of making the best decision for you.

# CHAPTER ONE

# What Are Your Early Retirement Benefits and Penalties?

This book will guide you through the seven key steps to help you determine if early retirement makes sense for you. The first step to answering your $100,000 Question is to learn exactly what your Social Security benefits will be. Next, you will learn about the penalties for early retirement, and the financial risks of making the wrong early retirement decision. In this chapter, you will learn the options and their cost to you.

## YOUR SOCIAL SECURITY STATEMENT

In 1999 the SSA began mailing Social Security statements annually to all adults 25 and over about three months prior to their birthdays. In the statement, you receive an estimate of your benefits under the most current laws, and a record of your earnings upon which your benefits are based. If you do not have this statement, you need to get one. Call 800-772-1213 or go to *www.ssa.gov* and request a statement order form. Because this is sensitive personal information, it is not available online. You have to mail a form to the SSA and wait for a response in four to six weeks.

Your Social Security statement estimates what your benefits will be based on current law and your history of earnings. As you get closer to retirement age the estimate of your benefits are more accurate, as your earning record is more complete and the laws are less apt to change. Check your earnings history to make sure it agrees with your records. The SSA estimates that employers submit incorrect information 4 percent of the time and it tries to correct most of the errors, but it estimates that 1 percent of wages fail to be credited to the correct worker's record. Nancy actually found an error several years ago. Those mistakes can cost you thousands. The most common mistakes occur because the SSA computer does not recognize your family name. Problems occur with hyphenated names, names with spaces, such as Oscar de la Hoya, and Asian and Spanish names in which the primary family name does not come at the end, such as Ho Zheng Fuhu and José López Portillo Alvarez.

In order to qualify for retirement benefits, you must have paid into the system and earned a minimum forty quarterly "work credits" or approximately ten years of work. You must earn at least $920 in a quarter, or $3,680 for the year [2005], to accumulate four annual credits. This amount is indexed upward each year for inflation. Spouses and dependents who are entitled to receive benefits based on your record of earnings credits do not have an earnings requirement themselves.

How do you calculate your benefits? Follow me through this three-step process. First, we will adjust earnings for inflation, then determine lifetime average earnings, and finally calculate benefits based on your average earnings.

First, let's find out your lifetime earnings adjusted for inflation. Each year of your earnings is adjusted forward based on real wage growth inflation to the Base Year that you turn 60. The inflation rate of wages is considerably more than what we commonly think as inflation as measured by the Consumer

Price Index (CPI) for Urban Wage Earners and Clerical Workers computed by the Bureau of Labor Statistics. The CPI measures inflation as experienced by consumers in their day-to-day living expenses. Fortunately for all of us, using the larger wage inflation factor creates a larger initial benefit the first year and therefore creates a larger stream of benefits thereafter with the larger initial base.

After you begin receiving benefits they are adjusted annually for inflation by using the lower CPI measure. In 2005 there was a 2.7 percent increase in benefits, the highest being 14.3 percent in 1980 a, and the lowest 1.3 percent in 1999. Fewer than 20 percent of private pensions have automatic cost-of-living increases, according to the Employee Benefit Research Institute, making Social Security very valuable in times of inflation.

Second, the SSA chooses the best thirty-five years of your adjusted earnings years to arrive at your benefits. Some people may have a few years of unemployment, child rearing, or education in their work records. Those zeros in your record reduce your benefits if they are part of your highest 35 years.

This total adjusted earnings amount is divided by 420, the number of months in 35 years, to determine your Average Indexed Monthly Earnings (AIME). You may have zeros in some years and that brings down your average. If you choose to retire early, you could be reducing your average by foregoing some of the highest paid years of your career in the calculation.

Once your AIME is calculated, the SSA applies a percentage, called a Replacement Rate, to arrive at your monthly benefits amount. The average Replacement Rate is 40 percent. However, the rate tends to be higher for low-income workers and lower for higher income workers. In this progressive way, lower-paid workers—who in theory would have less opportunity to save—get proportionally more of their incomes replaced by Social Security. A very low-paid worker may have a 90 percent replacement rate, yet receive a much smaller check. An upper income worker may only have a 33 percent replacement rate, but get a check three times as large in absolute terms. It is also not totally a progressive system because the maximum income subject to the Social Security tax is $90,000 [in 2005], which is adjusted upward annually for inflation. This leaves a large proportion of high earners' incomes untaxed.

By using the benefit-estimating Quick Calculator provided by the SSA at *www.ssa.gov,* I've developed the following charts showing approximate benefits for people with birthdays beginning in 1943, who can choose to collect an early retirement benefit beginning in 2005. The charts, not available anywhere else, input a range of incomes at the various birth years from 1943 to the present. The Quick Calculator assumes that you continue to work until retirement to estimate your benefits.

Your personal statement will give a more accurate picture because your earnings stream may differ from the average. Your personal statement will state what your early retirement benefit will be at age 62, what your full retirement benefit at your NRA, and what your benefits would be if you postpone benefits until age 70. Because of the changes in the Social Security law in 1983, the NRA is gradually increasing from age 65 currently to age 67 for those born in 1960 and thereafter. Surprisingly, half of us Baby Boomers don't know that. Legislators spared current and near retirees the pain of the corrective actions to save the system from insolvency. Those long-ago changes to benefits made in 1983 are starting to affect retirees today.

One reason the decisions you make regarding Social Security are so important is that these benefits are a major source of income support for most Americans. Although Social Security benefits were never intended to replace one's working income, they now keep millions and millions of retirees out of poverty, or contribute a major chunk of their annual incomes. Despite the wealth of the U.S. economy and the relative affluence of

## ESTIMATES OF YOUR SOCIAL SECURITY BENEFITS BY YEAR OF BIRTH

### Years of Birth 1943–1954
*Approximate Benefits*

| Income | Age 62 2005–2017 Early | Age 66 2009–2021 NRA | Age 70 2013–2025 Late |
|---|---|---|---|
| $20,000 | $545 | $754 | $1,033 |
| $25,000 | $616 | $855 | $1,174 |
| $30,000 | $685 | $955 | $1,316 |
| $35,000 | $755 | $1,055 | $1,457 |
| $40,000 | $824 | $1,154 | $1,598 |
| $45,000 | $894 | $1,255 | $1,740 |
| $50,000 | $964 | $1,355 | $1,881 |
| $55,000 | $1,033 | $1,455 | $2,022 |
| $65,000 | $1,165 | $1,591 | $2,157 |
| $75,000 | $1,230 | $1,685 | $2,289 |
| $85,000 | $1,295 | $1,779 | $2,422 |
| $100,000 | $1,373 | $1,881 | $2,547 |
| $125,000 | $1,419 | $1,942 | $2,626 |
| $150,000 | $1,419 | $1,942 | $2,626 |
| $200,000 | $1,419 | $1,942 | $2,626 |

### Year of Birth 1955
*Approximate Benefits*

| Income | Age 62 2017 Early | Age 66+2m 2021 NRA | Age 70 2025 Late |
|---|---|---|---|
| $20,000 | $602 | $830 | $1,110 |
| $25,000 | $687 | $949 | $1,272 |
| $30,000 | $772 | $1,068 | $1,433 |
| $35,000 | $856 | $1,187 | $1,596 |
| $40,000 | $941 | $1,306 | $1,757 |
| $45,000 | $1,025 | $1,425 | $1,919 |
| $50,000 | $1,110 | $1,539 | $2,041 |
| $55,000 | $1,168 | $1,595 | $2,117 |
| $65,000 | $1,247 | $1,707 | $2,268 |
| $75,000 | $1,327 | $1,818 | $2,420 |
| $85,000 | $1,406 | $1,930 | $2,572 |
| $100,000 | $1,470 | $2,007 | $2,659 |
| $125,000 | $1,507 | $2,037 | $2,678 |
| $150,000 | $1,507 | $2,037 | $2,678 |
| $200,000 | $1,507 | $2,037 | $2,678 |

### Year of Birth 1956
*Approximate Benefits*

| Income | Age 62 2018 Early | Age 66+4m 2022 NRA | Age 70 2026 Late |
|---|---|---|---|
| $20,000 | $600 | $835 | $1,104 |
| $25,000 | $685 | $956 | $1,266 |
| $30,000 | $769 | $1,076 | $1,427 |
| $35,000 | $854 | $1,196 | $1,589 |
| $40,000 | $939 | $1,316 | $1,750 |
| $45,000 | $1,024 | $1,437 | $1,912 |
| $50,000 | $1,108 | $1,454 | $2,027 |
| $55,000 | $1,160 | $1,602 | $2,102 |
| $65,000 | $1,240 | $1,714 | $2,254 |
| $75,000 | $1,319 | $1,827 | $2,405 |
| $85,000 | $1,399 | $1,940 | $2,556 |
| $100,000 | $1,461 | $2,015 | $2,639 |
| $125,000 | $1,494 | $2,040 | $2,655 |
| $150,000 | $1,494 | $2,040 | $2,655 |
| $200,000 | $1,494 | $2,040 | $2,655 |

### Year of Birth 1957
*Approximate Benefits*

| Income | Age 62 2019 Early | Age 66+6m 2023 NRA | Age 70 2027 Late |
|---|---|---|---|
| $20,000 | $597 | $840 | $1,098 |
| $25,000 | $682 | $962 | $1,260 |
| $30,000 | $767 | $1,083 | $1,420 |
| $35,000 | $852 | $1,205 | $1,582 |
| $40,000 | $936 | $1,326 | $1,742 |
| $45,000 | $1,021 | $1,448 | $1,904 |
| $50,000 | $1,106 | $1,551 | $2,012 |
| $55,000 | $1,153 | $1,608 | $2,087 |
| $65,000 | $1,232 | $1,722 | $2,238 |
| $75,000 | $1,312 | $1,836 | $2,390 |
| $85,000 | $1,391 | $1,950 | $2,540 |
| $100,000 | $1,451 | $2,022 | $2,619 |
| $125,000 | $1,480 | $2,043 | $2,632 |
| $150,000 | $1,480 | $2,043 | $2,632 |
| $200,000 | $1,480 | $2,043 | $2,632 |

*continued*

### Year of Birth 1958
*Approximate Benefits*

| Income | Age 62 2020 Early | Age 66 + 8 m 2025 NRA | Age 70 2028 Late |
|---|---|---|---|
| $20,000 | $594 | $850 | $1,091 |
| $25,000 | $679 | $973 | $1,252 |
| $30,000 | $764 | $1,097 | $1,413 |
| $35,000 | $849 | $1,221 | $1,574 |
| $40,000 | $934 | $1,345 | $1,734 |
| $45,000 | $1,019 | $1,468 | $1,895 |
| $50,000 | $1,104 | $1,562 | $1,997 |
| $55,000 | $1,145 | $1,620 | $2,072 |
| $65,000 | $1,224 | $1,736 | $2,223 |
| $75,000 | $1,304 | $1,852 | $2,373 |
| $85,000 | $1,383 | $1,968 | $2,524 |
| $100,000 | $1,441 | $2,035 | $2,597 |
| $125,000 | $1,465 | $2,050 | $2,608 |
| $150,000 | $1,465 | $2,050 | $2,608 |
| $200,000 | $1,465 | $2,050 | $2,608 |

### Year of Birth 1959
*Approximate Benefits*

| Income | Age 62 2021 Early | Age 66 + 10 m 2026 NRA | Age 70 2029 Late |
|---|---|---|---|
| $20,000 | $591 | $854 | $1,084 |
| $25,000 | $676 | $979 | $1,245 |
| $30,000 | $761 | $1,104 | $1,405 |
| $35,000 | $846 | $1,229 | $1,565 |
| $40,000 | $930 | $1,353 | $1,725 |
| $45,000 | $1,015 | $1,478 | $1,885 |
| $50,000 | $1,097 | $1,567 | $1,981 |
| $55,000 | $1,136 | $1,626 | $2,056 |
| $65,000 | $1,216 | $1,743 | $2,206 |
| $75,000 | $1,295 | $1,860 | $2,356 |
| $85,000 | $1,375 | $1,977 | $2,506 |
| $100,000 | $1,430 | $2,041 | $2,575 |
| $125,000 | $1,451 | $2,053 | $2,584 |
| $150,000 | $1,451 | $2,053 | $2,584 |
| $200,000 | $1,451 | $2,053 | $2,584 |

### Years of Birth 1960 and later
*Approximate Benefits*

| Income | Age 62 2022+ Early | Age 67 2027+ NRA | Age 70 2030+ Late |
|---|---|---|---|
| $20,000 | $588 | $858 | $1,077 |
| $25,000 | $673 | $984 | $1,237 |
| $30,000 | $758 | $1,110 | $1,396 |
| $35,000 | $842 | $1,236 | $1,556 |
| $40,000 | $927 | $1,361 | $1,715 |
| $45,000 | $1,012 | $1,487 | $1,874 |
| $50,000 | $1,088 | $1,572 | $1,965 |
| $55,000 | $1,128 | $1,631 | $2,039 |
| $65,000 | $1,207 | $1,749 | $2,189 |
| $75,000 | $1,287 | $1,867 | $2,338 |
| $85,000 | $1,366 | $1,985 | $2,488 |
| $100,000 | $1,418 | $2,046 | $2,552 |
| $125,000 | $1,436 | $2,056 | $2,560 |
| $150,000 | $1,436 | $2,056 | $2,560 |
| $200,000 | $1,436 | $2,056 | $2,560 |

the U.S. consumer, Social Security is rapidly becoming the only guaranteed retirement provided to American workers and their families. In fact, Social Security is the sole source of income for 18 percent of American retirees today, and it provides nine tenths of total income for almost a third of today's retirees. For 64 percent of current retirees, the Social Security check amounts to 50 percent of their income!

Enormous changes in the ways corporations provide retirement benefits to workers, and in the reliability of those benefits over long periods of time, have left each of us with far greater responsibility for planning and managing our finances in retirement than we would have thought possible even twenty years ago. Today, employers provide defined pension benefits plans (guaranteeing a set pension check amount to the retiree) to just 20 percent of current workers. And that number is expected to rapidly dwindle as employers continue to choose defined contribution plans, such as 401(k) plans, which establish retirement stock and savings accounts for employees who are responsible for managing their own assets. What's more, pension benefit cutbacks are becoming routine for troubled companies and industries. We're even reading reports in the *Wall Street Journal* that companies are hiring sheriffs to deliver retirees a summons with the news that their pension benefits are being slashed or eliminated!

The decline in traditional pensions is also due to the dwindling number of union employees who have guaranteed pension plans as part of their contracts. Approximately 80 percent of workers are now offered a defined contribution plan such as a 401(k), and are responsible for their contribution and investment choices, which may or may not provide an adequate retirement nest egg. Even the federal government has switched to a less costly plan. Employees hired after 1984 are part of the Social Security system rather than the more generous Federal Employee Plan.

| Nearly Two Thirds of Recipients Rely on Social Security for More Than 50% of Their Support | | |
|---|---|---|
| % of Support | % of Recipients | % Greater than or Equal |
| 100 | 18 | |
| 90 | 12 | 30 |
| 50 | 34 | 64 |

Source: SSA

## EARLY RETIREMENT

Retiring early: it's a huge topic of conversation, a staple of financial news stories, and a dream for many hard working midlifers paying that mortgage and saving for college tuition who hope to buy that log-hewn mountain house for their golden years. But few have realized just how big the price tag can be.

The typical working Baby Boomer stands to lose as much as 30 percent of his or her Social Security check by retiring early. A common misunderstanding is that the reduction for early retirement affects just the early retirement years. In fact, the reductions for early retirement are permanent and last throughout your retirement. I have created a chart (see page 9) that combines several sources of key information from the SSA, to help us understand how this works.

Let's take my brother Richard as an example. He was born in 1957, and his Social Security statement says that he is entitled to a monthly income of $2,022 per month at his FRA of 66 years and 6 months. Looking across the chart at his birth year of 1957, he turns 62 in 2019. His early benefit would be 72.5 percent of his full benefit (an early retirement penalty of 27.5 percent). When he is 66 and 6 months in 2023 he will reach his full retirement age.

## EARLY AND FULL RETIREMENT OPTIONS

| Year of Birth | Early Retirement Year at Age 62 | % Early Benefits of Full Benefits | % Reduction for Early Election | Full or Normal Retirement Age | NRA Year |
|---|---|---|---|---|---|
| 1941 | 2003 | 76.66% | 23.34% | 65 + 8 mos. | 2006–7 |
| 1942 | 2004 | 75.83% | 24.17% | 65 + 10 mos. | 2007–8 |
| 1943 | 2005 | 75.00% | 25.00% | 66 | 2009 |
| 1944 | 2006 | 75.00% | 25.00% | 66 | 2010 |
| 1945 | 2007 | 75.00% | 25.00% | 66 | 2011 |
| 1946 | 2008 | 75.00% | 25.00% | 66 | 2012 |
| 1947 | 2009 | 75.00% | 25.00% | 66 | 2013 |
| 1948 | 2010 | 75.00% | 25.00% | 66 | 2014 |
| 1949 | 2011 | 75.00% | 25.00% | 66 | 2015 |
| 1950 | 2012 | 75.00% | 25.00% | 66 | 2016 |
| 1951 | 2013 | 75.00% | 25.00% | 66 | 2017 |
| 1952 | 2014 | 75.00% | 25.00% | 66 | 2018 |
| 1953 | 2015 | 75.00% | 25.00% | 66 | 2019 |
| 1954 | 2016 | 75.00% | 25.00% | 66 | 2020 |
| 1955 | 2017 | 74.16% | 25.84% | 66 + 2 mos. | 2021–2 |
| 1956 | 2018 | 73.33% | 26.67% | 66 + 4 mos. | 2022–3 |
| **1957** | **2019** | **72.50%** | **27.50%** | **66 + 6 mos.** | **2023–4** |
| 1958 | 2020 | 71.66% | 28.34% | 66 + 8 mos. | 2024–5 |
| 1959 | 2021 | 70.83% | 29.17% | 66 + 10 mos. | 2025–6 |
| 1960 + | 2022 + | 70.00% | 30.00% | 67 | 2026 + |

*Early retirement reductions do not take into account taxes or penalties for earnings and other factors outlined in the book.*

## RETIRE EARLY AT 62—OR LATER

You can retire early at 62 with a penalty. You can also retire in the years between the earliest retirement dates and full retirement and get a bit more money with each passing year. Suppose you create a financial plan based upon the three-legged financial stool of personal savings, part-time income, and Social Security benefits. As your planned-for retirement date approaches, the stock market may crash, your employer's pension plan may default, or your retirement needs may appear to be considerably more than your financial planner had envisioned for you. You have the option to delay early retirement, but without waiting until your full retirement age.

You can also reconsider your plan and retire at the official full retirement date or even keep working past your full retirement age, until age 70—and get much more. The "Retirement Benefits for Early, Full, and Late Retirement" chart that follows brings all the possibilities together for you.

Take Richard's case. He was born in 1957. He would take his full retirement benefit figure and multiply it by the factor on the chart corresponding to the age at which he wants to retire. If he wanted to retire a little past the earliest possible age at 64, he would collect $1,684 a month ($2,022 × 83.33 percent). If he wanted to delay until 70, he would get 28 percent more than the full benefit or $2,588 ($2,022 × 128 percent).

## RETIREMENT BENEFITS FOR EARLY, FULL, AND LATE RETIREMENT

| Year of Birth | Full or Normal Retirement Age (NRA) | Credit for Each Year of Delay Past NRA | Benefits as a % of Full Benefits Age 62 | 63 | 64 | 65 | 66 | 67 | 70 |
|---|---|---|---|---|---|---|---|---|---|
| 1941 | 65 + 8 mos. | 7.5% | 76.66% | 82.22% | 88.88% | 95.55% | 102.50% | 110.00% | 132.50% |
| 1942 | 65 + 10 mos. | 7.5% | 75.83% | 81.11% | 87.77% | 94.44% | 101.25% | 108.75% | 131.25% |
| 1943 | 66 | 8% | 75% | 80% | 86.66% | 93.33% | 100% | 108% | 132% |
| 1944 | 66 | 8% | 75% | 80% | 86.66% | 93.33% | 100% | 108% | 132% |
| 1945 | 66 | 8% | 75% | 80% | 86.66% | 93.33% | 100% | 108% | 132% |
| 1946 | 66 | 8% | 75% | 80% | 86.66% | 93.33% | 100% | 108% | 132% |
| 1947 | 66 | 8% | 75% | 80% | 86.66% | 93.33% | 100% | 108% | 132% |
| 1948 | 66 | 8% | 75% | 80% | 86.66% | 93.33% | 100% | 108% | 132% |
| 1949 | 66 | 8% | 75% | 80% | 86.66% | 93.33% | 100% | 108% | 132% |
| 1950 | 66 | 8% | 75% | 80% | 86.66% | 93.33% | 100% | 100% | 132% |
| 1951 | 66 | 8% | 75% | 80% | 86.66% | 93.33% | 100% | 108% | 132% |
| 1952 | 66 | 8% | 75% | 80% | 86.66% | 93.33% | 100% | 108% | 132% |
| 1953 | 66 | 8% | 75% | 80% | 86.66% | 93.33% | 100% | 108% | 132% |
| 1954 | 66 | 8% | 75% | 80% | 86.66% | 93.33% | 100% | 108% | 132% |
| 1955 | 66 + 2 mos. | 8% | 74.16% | 79.16% | 85.55% | 92.22% | 98.88% | 106.66% | 130.66% |
| 1956 | 66 + 4 mos. | 8% | 73.33% | 78.33% | 84.44% | 91.11% | 97.77% | 105.33% | 129.33% |
| 1957 | 66 + 6 mos. | 8% | 72.50% | 77.50% | 83.33% | 90% | 96.66% | 104% | 128% |

| 1958 | 66 + 8 mos. | 8% | 71.66% | 76.66% | 82.22% | 88.88% | 95.55% | 102.66% | 126.66% |
| 1959 | 66 + 10 mos. | 8% | 70.83% | 75.83% | 81.11% | 87.77% | 94.44% | 101.33% | 125.33% |
| 1960 | +67 | 8% | 70% | 75% | 80% | 86.66% | 93.33% | 100% | 124% |

In addition to a penalty for early retirement, there is a credit for delaying retiring past your NRA until age 70.

Early retirement reductions do not take into account taxes or penalties for earnings and other factors outlined in the book.

That sounds very straightforward. Take your birth year and make your choice of what you want to do. But it is not that simple. If it were so easy this book would not exist. You want to know how to get the most out of the system for your particular circumstances. You can wait and get more per month, but if you choose reduced benefits early, you would be collecting for three to five more years. At what point do you start collecting more by waiting? That is called the "break-even point."

## THE BREAK-EVEN POINT

Using the Quick Calculator that estimated the benefits, you can find out the ages at which you break even waiting for your benefits. If you live and collect benefits for a longer period than the breakeven, you are ahead of the game financially because you will collect more benefits in your lifetime. But more importantly, you will have lived longer.

Continuing with my brother Richard's example, he will look at the chart on page 14 for the year 1957. Again, I created these charts by using the SSA Quick Calculator for a variety of incomes to make it easier for you. Look at Richard's current income and birth year on the 1957 chart to see the approximate benefits he will receive. He would break even waiting for his full retirement instead of taking an early check if he lives beyond 77 years and 8 months. Beyond that point the higher benefits for waiting will be more than the early benefits received. If he waits for higher benefits available for delaying retirement until age 70, rather than taking early retirement benefits, Richard has a break-even age of 79 years and 10 months.

Or look at one last break-even scenario: what he gets taking full retirement at NRA versus waiting until age 70. In this case, the break-even age is 81 years and 10 months. Few people do this, but it is a possibility. Take these break-even ages with a grain of salt, as they do not account for penalties and taxes for earnings during early retirement as explained in later chapters that may apply to you.

## BREAK-EVEN AGES AND BENEFITS FOR EARLY, FULL, AND LATE RETIREMENT

### Years of Birth 1943–1954

| | Approximate Benefits | | | Break-even Ages | | |
|---|---|---|---|---|---|---|
| | Age 62 2005–2017 | Age 66 2009–2021 | Age 70 2013–2025 | | | |
| Income | Early | NRA | Late | Early vs. NRA | Early vs. Late | NRA vs. Late |
| $20,000 | $545 | $754 | $1,033 | 76 years 2 mos. | 78 years 10 mos. | 80 years 9 mos. |
| $25,000 | $616 | $855 | $1,174 | 76 years 1 mos. | 78 years 8 mos. | 80 years 8 mos. |
| $30,000 | $685 | $955 | $1,316 | 75 years 11 mos. | 78 years 7 mos. | 80 years 6 mos. |
| $35,000 | $755 | $1,055 | $1,457 | 75 years 10 mos. | 78 years 6 mos. | 80 years 5 mos. |
| $40,000 | $824 | $1,154 | $1,598 | 75 years 9 mos. | 78 years 5 mos. | 80 years 4 mos. |
| $45,000 | $894 | $1,255 | $1,740 | 75 years 8 mos. | 78 years 4 mos. | 80 years 4 mos. |
| $50,000 | $964 | $1,355 | $1,881 | 75 years 7 mos. | 78 years 3 mos. | 80 years 3 mos. |
| $55,000 | $1,033 | $1,455 | $2,022 | 75 years 7 mos. | 78 years 3 mos. | 80 years 3 mos. |
| $65,000 | $1,165 | $1,591 | $2,157 | 76 years 8 mos. | 79 years 3 mos. | 81 years 2 mos. |
| $75,000 | $1,230 | $1,685 | $2,289 | 76 years 7 mos. | 79 years 2 mos. | 81 years 1 mos. |
| $85,000 | $1,295 | $1,779 | $2,422 | 76 years 5 mos. | 79 years 1 mos. | 81 years 0 mos. |
| $100,000 | $1,373 | $1,881 | $2,547 | 76 years 7 mos. | 79 years 3 mos. | 81 years 3 mos. |
| $125,000 | $1,419 | $1,942 | $2,626 | 76 years 7 mos. | 79 years 3 mos. | 81 years 4 mos. |
| $150,000 | $1,419 | $1,942 | $2,626 | 76 years 7 mos. | 79 years 3 mos. | 81 years 4 mos. |
| $200,000 | $1,419 | $1,942 | $2,626 | 76 years 7 mos. | 79 years 3 mos. | 81 years 4 mos. |

## Year of Birth 1955

| Approximate Benefits | | | Break-even Ages | | |
|---|---|---|---|---|---|
| Age 62 2017 | Age 66 + 2 mos. 2021 | Age 70 2025 | | | |
| **Income** **Early** | **NRA** | **Late** | **Early vs. NRA** | **Early vs. Late** | **NRA vs. Late** |
| $20,000 $602 | $830 | $1,110 | 76 years 11 mos. | 79 years 4 mos. | 81 years 4 mos. |
| $25,000 $687 | $949 | $1,272 | 76 years 10 mos. | 79 years 3 mos. | 81 years 3 mos. |
| $30,000 $772 | $1,068 | $1,433 | 76 years 9 mos. | 79 years 2 mos. | 81 years 2 mos. |
| $35,000 $856 | $1,187 | $1,596 | 76 years 8 mos. | 79 years 1 mos. | 81 years 1 mos. |
| $40,000 $941 | $1,306 | $1,757 | 76 years 8 mos. | 79 years 1 mos. | 81 years 1 mos. |
| $45,000 $1,025 | $1,425 | $1,919 | 76 years 7 mos. | 79 years 0 mos. | 81 years 0 mos. |
| $50,000 $1,110 | $1,539 | $2,041 | 76 years 8 mos. | 79 years 5 mos. | 81 years 9 mos. |
| $55,000 $1,168 | $1,595 | $2,117 | 77 years 4 mos. | 79 years 8 mos. | 81 years 8 mos. |
| $65,000 $1,247 | $1,707 | $2,268 | 77 years 2 mos. | 79 years 8 mos. | 81 years 7 mos. |
| $75,000 $1,327 | $1,818 | $2,420 | 77 years 2 mos. | 79 years 7 mos. | 81 years 6 mos. |
| $85,000 $1,406 | $1,930 | $2,572 | 77 years 1 mos. | 79 years 6 mos. | 81 years 6 mos. |
| $100,000 $1,470 | $2,007 | $2,659 | 77 years 4 mos. | 79 years 9 mos. | 81 years 9 mos. |
| $125,000 $1,507 | $2,037 | $2,678 | 77 years 9 mos. | 80 years 2 mos. | 82 years 2 mos. |
| $150,000 $1,507 | $2,037 | $2,678 | 77 years 9 mos. | 80 years 2 mos. | 82 years 2 mos. |
| $200,000 $1,507 | $2,037 | $2,678 | 77 years 9 mos. | 80 years 2 mos. | 82 years 2 mos. |

## Year of Birth 1956

| Approximate Benefits | | | Break-even Ages | | |
|---|---|---|---|---|---|
| Age 62 2018 | Age 66 + 4 mos. 2022 | Age 70 2026 | | | |
| **Income** **Early** | **NRA** | **Late** | **Early vs. NRA** | **Early vs. Late** | **NRA vs. Late** |
| $20,000 $600 | $835 | $1,104 | 77 years 2 mos. | 79 years 5 mos. | 81 years 4 mos. |
| $25,000 $685 | $956 | $1,266 | 77 years 0 mos. | 79 years 4 mos. | 81 years 3 mos. |
| $30,000 $769 | $1,076 | $1,427 | 76 years 11 mos. | 79 years 3 mos. | 81 years 2 mos. |
| $35,000 $854 | $1,196 | $1,509 | 76 years 11 mos. | 79 years 2 mos. | 81 years 1 mos. |
| $40,000 $939 | $1,316 | $1,750 | 76 years 11 mos. | 79 years 1 mos. | 81 years 1 mos. |
| $45,000 $1,024 | $1,437 | $1,912 | 76 years 10 mos. | 79 years 1 mos. | 81 years 1 mos. |
| $50,000 $1,108 | $1,454 | $2,027 | 77 years 1 mos. | 79 years 6 mos. | 81 years 9 mos. |
| $55,000 $1,160 | $1,602 | $2,102 | 77 years 5 mos. | 79 years 8 mos. | 81 years 8 mos. |
| $65,000 $1,240 | $1,714 | $2,254 | 77 years 5 mos. | 79 years 8 mos. | 81 years 7 mos. |
| $75,000 $1,319 | $1,827 | $2,405 | 77 years 4 mos. | 79 years 7 mos. | 81 years 7 mos. |
| $85,000 $1,399 | $1,940 | $2,556 | 77 years 3 mos. | 79 years 6 mos. | 81 years 6 mos. |
| $100,000 $1,461 | $2,015 | $2,639 | 77 years 6 mos. | 79 years 9 mos. | 81 years 10 mos. |
| $125,000 $1,494 | $2,040 | $2,655 | 77 years 11 mos. | 80 years 2 mos. | 82 years 1 mos. |
| $150,000 $1,494 | $2,040 | $2,655 | 77 years 11 mos. | 80 years 2 mos. | 82 years 1 mos. |
| $200,000 $1,494 | $2,040 | $2,655 | 77 years 11 mos. | 80 years 2 mos. | 82 years 1 mos. |

*continued*

## Year of Birth 1957 (Rich's)

| | Approximate Benefits | | | Break-even Ages | | |
|---|---|---|---|---|---|---|
| | Age 62 2019 | Age 66 + 6 mos. 2023 | Age 70 2027 | | | |
| Income | Early | NRA | Late | Early vs. NRA | Early vs. Late | NRA vs. Late |
| $20,000 | $597 | $840 | $1,098 | 77 years 4 mos. | 79 years 5 mos. | 81 years 4 mos. |
| $25,000 | $682 | $962 | $1,260 | 77 years 3 mos. | 79 years 4 mos. | 81 years 3 mos. |
| $30,000 | $767 | $1,083 | $1,420 | 77 years 2 mos. | 79 years 3 mos. | 81 years 2 mos. |
| $35,000 | $852 | $1,205 | $1,582 | 77 years 1 mos. | 79 years 2 mos. | 81 years 2 mos. |
| $40,000 | $936 | $1,326 | $1,742 | 77 years 1 mos. | 79 years 2 mos. | 81 years 1 mos. |
| $45,000 | $1,021 | $1,448 | $1,904 | 77 years 0 mos. | 79 years 1 mos. | 81 years 1 mos. |
| $50,000 | $1,106 | $1,551 | $2,012 | 77 years 5 mos. | 79 years 7 mos. | 81 years 9 mos. |
| $55,000 | $1,153 | $1,608 | $2,087 | 77 years 8 mos. | 79 years 9 mos. | 81 years 8 mos. |
| $65,000 | $1,232 | $1,722 | $2,238 | 77 years 7 mos. | 79 years 8 mos. | 81 years 8 mos. |
| $75,000 | $1,312 | $1,836 | $2,390 | 77 years 6 mos. | 79 years 7 mos. | 81 years 7 mos. |
| $85,000 | $1,391 | $1,950 | $2,540 | 77 years 5 mos. | 79 years 7 mos. | 81 years 6 mos. |
| **$100,000** | **$1,451** | **$2,022** | **$2,619** | **77 years 8 mos.** | **79 years 10 mos.** | **81 years 10 mos.** |
| $125,000 | $1,480 | $2,043 | $2,632 | 78 years 1 mos. | 80 years 2 mos. | 82 years 1 mos. |
| $150,000 | $1,480 | $2,043 | $2,632 | 78 years 1 mos. | 80 years 2 mos. | 82 years 1 mos. |
| $200,000 | $1,480 | $2,043 | $2,632 | 78 years 1 mos. | 80 years 2 mos. | 82 years 1 mos. |

## Year of Birth 1958

| | Approximate Benefits | | | Break-even Ages | | |
|---|---|---|---|---|---|---|
| | Age 62 2020 | Age 66 + 8 mos. 2025 | Age 70 2028 | | | |
| Income | Early | NRA | Late | Early vs. NRA | Early vs. Late | NRA vs. Late |
| $20,000 | $594 | $850 | $1,091 | 77 years 3 mos. | 79 years 5 mos. | 81 years 9 mos. |
| $25,000 | $679 | $973 | $1,252 | 77 years 3 mos. | 79 years 4 mos. | 81 years 7 mos. |
| $30,000 | $764 | $1,097 | $1,413 | 77 years 2 mos. | 79 years 3 mos. | 81 years 6 mos. |
| $35,000 | $849 | $1,221 | $1,574 | 77 years 1 mos. | 79 years 3 mos. | 81 years 6 mos. |
| $40,000 | $934 | $1,345 | $1,734 | 77 years 0 mos. | 79 years 2 mos. | 81 years 6 mos. |
| $45,000 | $1,019 | $1,468 | $1,895 | 77 years 0 mos. | 79 years 2 mos. | 81 years 5 mos. |
| $50,000 | $1,104 | $1,562 | $1,997 | 77 years 8 mos. | 79 years 9 mos. | 81 years 11 mos. |
| $55,000 | $1,145 | $1,620 | $2,072 | 77 years 8 mos. | 79 years 9 mos. | 81 years 11 mos. |
| $65,000 | $1,224 | $1,736 | $2,223 | 77 years 7 mos. | 79 years 8 mos. | 81 years 10 mos. |
| $75,000 | $1,304 | $1,852 | $2,373 | 77 years 6 mos. | 79 years 7 mos. | 81 years 10 mos. |
| $85,000 | $1,383 | $1,968 | $2,524 | 77 years 6 mos. | 79 years 7 mos. | 81 years 9 mos. |
| $100,000 | $1,441 | $2,035 | $2,597 | 77 years 9 mos. | 79 years 10 mos. | 82 years 0 mos. |
| $125,000 | $1,465 | $2,050 | $2,608 | 78 years 1 mos. | 80 years 1 mos. | 82 years 2 mos. |
| $150,000 | $1,465 | $2,050 | $2,608 | 78 years 1 mos. | 80 years 1 mos. | 82 years 2 mos. |
| $200,000 | $1,465 | $2,050 | $2,608 | 78 years 1 mos. | 80 years 1 mos. | 82 years 2 mos. |

## Year of Birth 1959

| | Approximate Benefits | | | Break-even Ages | | |
|---|---|---|---|---|---|---|
| | Age 62 2021 | Age 66 + 10 mos. 2026 | Age 70 2029 | | | |
| **Income** | **Early** | **NRA** | **Late** | **Early vs. NRA** | **Early vs. Late** | **NRA vs. Late** |
| $20,000 | $591 | $854 | $1,084 | 77 years 6 mos. | 79 years 5 mos. | 81 years 9 mos. |
| $25,000 | $676 | $979 | $1,245 | 77 years 5 mos. | 79 years 4 mos. | 81 years 7 mos. |
| $30,000 | $761 | $1,104 | $1,405 | 77 years 4 mos. | 79 years 4 mos. | 81 years 7 mos. |
| $35,000 | $846 | $1,229 | $1,565 | 77 years 3 mos. | 79 years 3 mos. | 81 years 6 mos. |
| $40,000 | $930 | $1,353 | $1,725 | 77 years 3 mos. | 79 years 3 mos. | 81 years 6 mos. |
| $45,000 | $1,015 | $1,478 | $1,885 | 77 years 2 mos. | 79 years 2 mos. | 81 years 5 mos. |
| $50,000 | $1,097 | $1,567 | $1,981 | 77 years 11 mos. | 79 years 9 mos. | 81 years 11 mos. |
| $55,000 | $1,136 | $1,626 | $2,056 | 77 years 10 mos. | 79 years 9 mos. | 81 years 11 mos. |
| $65,000 | $1,216 | $1,743 | $2,206 | 77 years 9 mos. | 79 years 8 mos. | 81 years 11 mos. |
| $75,000 | $1,295 | $1,860 | $2,356 | 77 years 8 mos. | 79 years 7 mos. | 81 years 10 mos. |
| $85,000 | $1,375 | $1,977 | $2,506 | 77 years 8 mos. | 79 years 7 mos. | 81 years 10 mos. |
| $100,000 | $1,430 | $2,041 | $2,575 | 77 years 11 mos. | 79 years 10 mos. | 82 years 1 mos. |
| $125,000 | $1,451 | $2,053 | $2,584 | 78 years 3 mos. | 80 years 1 mos. | 82 years 2 mos. |
| $150,000 | $1,451 | $2,053 | $2,584 | 78 years 3 mos. | 80 years 1 mos. | 82 years 2 mos. |
| $200,000 | $1,451 | $2,053 | $2,584 | 78 years 3 mos. | 80 years 1 mos. | 82 years 2 mos. |

## Years of Birth 1960+

| | Approximate Benefits | | | Break-even Ages | | |
|---|---|---|---|---|---|---|
| | Age 62 2022+ | Age 67 2027+ | Age 70 2030+ | | | |
| **Income** | **Early** | **NRA** | **Late** | **Early vs. NRA** | **Early vs. Late** | **NRA vs. Late** |
| $20,000 | $588 | $858 | $1,077 | 77 years 8 mos. | 79 years 6 mos. | 81 years 9 mos. |
| $25,000 | $673 | $984 | $1,237 | 77 years 7 mos. | 79 years 5 mos. | 81 years 8 mos. |
| $30,000 | $758 | $1,110 | $1,396 | 77 years 7 mos. | 79 years 4 mos. | 81 years 7 mos. |
| $35,000 | $842 | $1,236 | $1,556 | 77 years 6 mos. | 79 years 4 mos. | 81 years 7 mos. |
| $40,000 | $927 | $1,361 | $1,715 | 77 years 6 mos. | 79 years 3 mos. | 81 years 6 mos. |
| $45,000 | $1,012 | $1,487 | $1,874 | 77 years 5 mos. | 79 years 3 mos. | 81 years 6 mos. |
| $50,000 | $1,088 | $1,572 | $1,965 | 78 years 0 mos. | 79 years 9 mos. | 81 years 11 mos. |
| $55,000 | $1,128 | $1,631 | $2,039 | 78 years 0 mos. | 79 years 9 mos. | 81 years 11 mos. |
| $65,000 | $1,207 | $1,749 | $2,189 | 77 years 11 mos. | 79 years 8 mos. | 81 years 11 mos. |
| $75,000 | $1,287 | $1,867 | $2,338 | 77 years 10 mos. | 79 years 8 mos. | 81 years 10 mos. |
| $85,000 | $1,366 | $1,985 | $2,488 | 77 years 10 mos. | 79 years 7 mos. | 81 years 10 mos. |
| $100,000 | $1,418 | $2,046 | $2,552 | 78 years 1 mos. | 79 years 10 mos. | 82 years 1 mos. |
| $125,000 | $1,436 | $2,056 | $2,560 | 78 years 4 mos. | 80 years 1 mos. | 82 years 2 mos. |
| $150,000 | $1,436 | $2,056 | $2,560 | 78 years 4 mos. | 80 years 1 mos. | 82 years 2 mos. |
| $200,000 | $1,436 | $2,056 | $2,560 | 78 years 4 mos. | 80 years 1 mos. | 82 years 2 mos. |

The charts show that my brother's breakeven age is 77 years and 8 months if he takes his benefits at NRA and not earlier. He will come out ahead only if he lives beyond 77 years and 8 months. That begs the thorny question, "How long am I projected to live?" That is the subject of the next chapter.

## Is a Decision Possible?
No. Knowing your benefits and breakevens are not enough. You need more information.

Please write down the information from your own Social Security statement so that you can move on to the next chapter and build toward your decision.

| | Early Retire at 62 | Full Retire NRA | Late Retire at 70 |
|---|---|---|---|
| Benefits Amount | | | |
| Break-even Ages | | | |

# CHAPTER TWO

# How's Your Health?

How's your health? How well is your spouse? How long do you both expect to live? The uncomfortable answers to these questions are very important factors to consider when making your early retirement decision. When you were a teenager and in your twenties, your life seemed limitless. You were invincible to perils of diseases, dangers, and age. You and I both thought to ourselves, "Those bad things will not happen to me, I'm special." However, as we Boomers have become wiser to the ways of the world we realize that we have our limits. If you have a reason to think that you have a shorter than average life ahead of you, you may want to "take it now rather than later." You may be in poor health or have a family history of poor health and short lives. If your family members have enjoyed long, productive lives, then waiting for larger benefits may be the best course. When I spoke to Nancy about the whole issue of longevity she became uncomfortable. We Boomers want to put off thinking about these things, but unfortunately you can't if you want to take control of your retirement future.

Longevity is determined by your lifestyle, your genetics, and perhaps fate. Although the debate rages about the effects of each, it is generally agreed that all three factors are important.

Let's refer to the rather unpleasant but informative guide published by the SSA called the Period Life Table. These tables show estimated life spans of millions of Americans. As you look at this table, you will notice that folks with older ages have longer life spans. That's because if you reach retirement age, you have lived through the illnesses and stresses of life, and have avoided deadly accidents. It is also because older people either have a better family history or have lived a healthier or safer lifestyle.

According to this table (next page), my brother can expect to reach the age of 80. Notice I did not choose the line for his current age, but I chose 62 because that is the age when he will make the early retirement decision.

Let's review my brother's break-even numbers as shown in his 1957 chart in the last chapter. If he takes early retirement, he will break even if he lives beyond 77 years and 8 months. If he waits until age 70 he will break even if he lives beyond 79 years and 10 months. If he retires at his NRA, then he will break even if he lives beyond 81 years and 10 months. At a quick glance, his breakevens are all close to his estimated life expectancy. And that is what the Social Security system intended. The benefits structure, based on actuarial tables, tries to be fair to all. Because the charts are based on averages, statistically one has a 50 percent chance of living longer, and a 50 percent chance of living a shorter life. That fact is an often overlooked one. That is why your personal assessment is necessary.

If you are married and planning for retirement, there is more than individual life span estimates to consider. There is a chart that estimates the Joint Life Expectancy of couples. When two people are involved, the projected life span is longer than for each individual. Maybe one looks after the other and spots illnesses early or forces the other to get a regular checkup and take his or her medicine. For instance, a couple at age 62 should

## LONGEVITY AT DIFFERENT AGES
### THE PERIOD LIFE TABLE

| At Age | Male Years Left | Death at Age | Female Years Left | Death at Age |
|--------|-----------------|--------------|-------------------|--------------|
| 40 | 36.43 | 76.43 | 40.85 | 80.85 |
| 41 | 35.52 | 76.52 | 39.91 | 80.91 |
| 42 | 34.62 | 76.62 | 38.98 | 80.98 |
| 43 | 33.73 | 76.73 | 38.04 | 81.04 |
| 44 | 32.84 | 76.84 | 37.11 | 81.11 |
| 45 | 31.95 | 76.95 | 36.19 | 81.19 |
| 46 | 31.08 | 77.08 | 35.26 | 81.26 |
| 47 | 30.21 | 77.21 | 34.34 | 81.34 |
| 48 | 29.34 | 77.34 | 33.43 | 81.43 |
| 49 | 28.48 | 77.48 | 32.52 | 81.52 |
| 50 | 27.63 | 77.63 | 31.61 | 81.61 |
| 51 | 26.78 | 77.78 | 30.71 | 81.71 |
| 52 | 25.93 | 77.93 | 29.81 | 81.81 |
| 53 | 25.09 | 78.09 | 28.92 | 81.92 |
| 54 | 24.26 | 78.26 | 28.04 | 82.04 |
| 55 | 23.44 | 78.44 | 27.16 | 82.16 |
| 56 | 22.63 | 78.63 | 26.30 | 82.30 |
| 57 | 21.83 | 78.83 | 25.44 | 82.44 |
| 58 | 21.04 | 79.04 | 24.59 | 82.59 |
| 59 | 20.26 | 79.26 | 23.75 | 82.75 |
| 60 | 19.49 | 79.49 | 22.92 | 82.92 |
| 61 | 18.73 | 79.73 | 22.10 | 83.10 |
| **62** | **17.99** | **79.99** | **21.29** | **83.29** |
| 63 | 17.25 | 80.25 | 20.49 | 83.49 |
| 64 | 16.54 | 80.54 | 19.70 | 83.70 |
| 65 | 15.84 | 80.84 | 18.93 | 83.93 |

*Source: Adapted from SSA data.*

consider 86.9 years as their joint life span. That age is significantly higher than the longest estimate for the woman alone.

| | | | JOINT LIFE EXPECTANCY | | | | |
|---|---|---|---|---|---|---|---|
| | | | | Female's Age | | | |
| | | 62 | 63 | 64 | 65 | 66 | 67 |
| Male's Age | 62 | 86.9 | | | | | |
| | 63 | | 87.0 | | | | |
| | 64 | | | 87.1 | | | |
| | 65 | | | | 87.3 | | |
| | 66 | | | | | 87.4 | |
| | 67 | | | | | | 87.6 |

Source: U.S. Life Tables, 2000.

The Society of Actuaries has taken a closer look at longevity (see next page). Actuaries study longevity statistics for insurance companies so that they can determine how much to charge for life insurance policies and still make money. The group takes a probabilistic view of life span, and estimates the chances to live past various ages. By judging the probability that you will live past a certain age, you can make a better estimate for your retirement decisions.

As we can see in comparing the chart on the next page with the Period Life Table, the Society of Actuaries projects longer life spans. (I like actuaries, don't you?) The last line of the Period Life Chart shows a man at age 65 with a projected life span of 15.8 years. Implicit in that projection is that there is a 50 percent chance he will live a longer or shorter life. The Actuaries' chart projects that a 65-year-old man has a 69 percent chance of living 15 years and a 50 percent chance of living 20 years. That would be an average life span of 85 years for a 65-year-old man versus

## PROBABILITIES OF LIVING LONG LIVES

### Chances of Living More Than:

| | 15 yrs. | 20 yrs. | 25 yrs. | 30 yrs. | 35 yrs. | 40 yrs. |
|---|---|---|---|---|---|---|
| **MEN** | | | | | | |
| Age 60 | 80% | 66% | 48% | 29% | 13% | 4% |
| Age 65 | 69% | 50% | 30% | 14% | 5% | 1% |
| Age 70 | 54% | 33% | 15% | 5% | 1% | 0% |
| | | | | | | |
| **WOMEN** | | | | | | |
| Age 60 | 87% | 77% | 62% | 41% | 20% | 7% |
| Age 65 | 79% | 63% | 42% | 20% | 7% | 1% |
| Age 70 | 66% | 44% | 21% | 7% | 1% | 0% |

Source: Society of Actuaries Annuity Table with Projection Scale G to 2002.

Assumes a healthy person at that age and gender retiring in 2003 and includes an estimate for medical improvements during the time period.

the Period Life Table projection of 80.84 years provided by the chart from the SSA. If you believe the more optimistic Actuaries' chart, you are apt to wait for the higher benefits.

## WHAT IS YOUR FAMILY CONNECTION?

Since genetics has a great deal to do with longevity, your family history is more important than any chart. Take my survey, on the next page, of your family's longevity. You may not know all the information, but fill in the ages of death that you do know. For those who are still living, place their age in parentheses for reference.

There is no scientific way to weight the ages, but by seeing them in one place you may be able to see a pattern to help you determine if the break-even year is a reasonable goal for yourself.

Your Mother _____
Your Brothers _____  Your Sisters _____

**Mother's Family**
Brothers _____  Sisters _____
Mother _____  Father_____
Uncles_____  Aunts _____
Grandfather _____  Grandmother_____

Your Father _____

**Father's Family**
Brothers _____  Sisters _____
Mother _____  Father_____
Uncles_____  Aunts _____
Grandfather _____  Grandmother_____

Let's use my brother again as an example.

Mother  73
Brother  (43)

**Mother's Family**
Brothers  (70)
Mother  81  Father  74
Uncles  43, 67, 88  Aunts  77
Grandfather  63  Grandmother  81

Father  60

**Father's Family**
Brothers  none  Sisters  none
Mother  84  Father  67
Uncles  71  Aunts  16, 75
Grandfather  82  Grandmother  88

No definitive answers arise from surveying the ages, but this exercise does provide a general picture of longevity in your genetic history. My family history does not seem to indicate exceptionally long life spans for my brother and me. So regrettably my brother and I can't assume that our genetic code will help him reach his break-even age of 77. But fortunately, medical science has advanced considerably in the last century, which might extend ours lives if we are faced with some of the same maladies as our forebears.

## LONGEVITY LIFESTYLE SURVEY

Other reliable surveys combine factors of family history and your lifestyle to arrive at an estimate of longevity. This exercise (below) may make you feel better if, like Richard's and mine, your family history is not filled with 100-year feats of aging. It focuses on activities over which you have some control. When I applied for life and disability insurance, the agent asked me if I participated in high-risk activities such as piloting aircraft, scuba diving, sky diving, unprotected sex, or intravenous drug use.

The following questionnaire is a bit more balanced because it takes into account both your family history and your lifestyle. Men begin with an age of 73 and women begin with age 80 on the survey. Depending on the factors you add or subtract years. Use the space provided with each factor to keep a running total.

| Lifestyle and Family Longevity Questionnaire |
| --- |

**Start:**

 Men start at 73 years, Women start at 80 years _____
 If you are in your 30s add 2 _____
 If you are in your 40s add 3 _____

If you are in your 50s add 4 _____
If you are in your 60s add 5 _____

### Family History Questions

If 2 or more grandparents lived past 80 years old,
add 4 _____

If a parent, grandparent, sister, or brother died of a heart
attack or stroke before 50, subtract 3 _____

If a parent, grandparent, sister, or brother died of a heart
attack or stroke before 60, subtract 2 _____

For each instance of juvenile diabetes, thyroid disorder,
breast cancer, cancer of the digestive system, or chronic bron-
chitis among parents and grandparents, subtract 3 each _____

### Marital Questions

Married? Add 4 _____

Living alone past the age of 25? Subtract 1 per
decade _____

### Economic Questions

Earn over $75,000? Add 2 _____

Poor most of your life? Subtract 3 _____

### Physical Questions

Overweight? Subtract 1 for every 10 pounds overweight
according to your doctor _____

Big-waisted? Subtract 2 for every inch your waist exceeds
your chest _____

Do you sleep for more than 10 hours a day?
Subtract 3 _____

### Exercise Questions

Do you walk, jog, run, play tennis, swim, etc. three times a
week? Add 3 _____

Sedentary job subtract 3 or add 3 for an active job _____

### Alcohol Questions

Light drinking (1 drink per day) add 3 _____
Heavy drinker of four drinks or more a day? Subtract 7 _____

### Smoking Questions

Smoke two packs a day or more? Subtract 8 _____
Smoke one to two packs a day? Subtract 6 _____
Smoke one pack or less a day? Subtract 3 _____

### Personality Questions

Are you a reasoned, practical person? Add 1 _____
Are you an aggressive, intense person? Subtract 2 _____
Are you basically a happy and content person?
Add 2 _____
Are you often unhappy, worried, and often feel guilty?
Subtract 2 _____

### Education Questions

If you did not complete high school, subtract 2 _____
Did you complete college? Add 1 _____
Graduate school? Add 2 _____

### Environmental Questions

Have you lived most of your life in a rural area?
Add 4 _____
Live in an urban area? Subtract 2 _____

### Health Care Questions

Do you get regular checkups and dental exams?
Add 3 _____

Are you frequently ill with various conditions?
Subtract 2 _____

Final total _____

Your total is your estimated longevity based on multiple factors. You can use this as another yardstick to estimate your longevity and gauge your chances of living past your break-even age. My brother's longevity looks much better in this test, since his age score of age 84 is based on his lifestyle and choices. I feel better too as I pretty much have the same lifestyle, short of his scuba diving and cave exploration hobbies. Considering this encouraging result, the decision to wait for benefits looks more reasonable to him.

An important issue for many who retire early at age 62 is continuing their health insurance. If you worked for a company with over 20 employees, you can continue on your employer's plan for a period of 18 months by paying for the full cost of the coverage under COBRA provisions in the law. However, after that coverage expires, you will have to purchase health insurance until you are eligible for Medicare at age 65. If you have a preexisting condition or have high-risk habits you may either not find coverage or may find it prohibitively expensive. Even if you are healthy it can be very costly, whether or not you choose a plan with a high deductible and high copays.

## LEADING HEALTH RISKS

The vast majority of deaths are due to health issues, not accidents, no matter what your mother told you. The National Center for Health Statistics compiles the list of killers. Some on the list you can't control but others you can. If you eat right, exercise, don't smoke, keep your weight under control, and manage your stress, you have a chance to minimize the leading causes of death. The best thing that you can do for your retirement is to take good care of yourself today. A study published in November 2004 by the University of Michigan Medical School and the VA Ann Arbor Health Care System found that adults in their 50s and 60s who were regularly active were 65 percent more likely to live eight additional years than those who were sedentary. The overwhelming favorite sporting activity for retirees is exercise walking, followed far behind by swimming, exercising with equipment, and golf, according to the National Sporting Goods Association.

## THE BIG KILLERS

### Estimated Leading Causes of Death

| Causes | Annual Deaths |
| --- | --- |
| Heart disease | 699,700 |
| Cancer | 553,300 |
| Stroke | 163,600 |
| Chronic lower respiratory disease | 124,000 |
| Accidents* | 97,700 |
| Diabetes | 71,300 |
| Pneumonia and influenza | 62,100 |
| Alzheimer's disease | 53,700 |
| Nephritis (kidney disease) | 39,700 |
| Septicemia (bacteria in blood) | 32,300 |

Source: National Center for Health Statistics, 2001.

* 42,000 were auto accident deaths, of which 17,000 were alcohol related. Source: National Highway Transportation Safety Administration.

The other way you can go is in an accident. So be careful. The government estimates the number of injuries requiring hospital visits from various types of accidents. I include my guess as to their nature in parentheses. Running with scissors, cramping in the pool after eating, and choking on food don't even rank. The real statistics tell us to avoid pillow fights, hammocks, and stairs to ensure a long, healthy retirement.

| KEEPING OUT OF THE EMERGENCY ROOM | | |
|---|---|---|
| **Accidents to Avoid** | | |
| **Stated Cause** | **Accidents** | **(Possible Causes)** |
| Stairs | 1,088,000 | Falling down and/or collapsing stairs |
| Nails, screws, and bolts | 179,800 | Professional craftsmen and tinkerers |
| Ramps and landings | 128,000 | Railing giving in, collapsing, wheelchairs |
| Books, magazines, and albums | 10,700 | Falling on you and lifting them |
| Pillows | 5,000 | Pillow fights |
| Crayons and chalk | 3,500 | Little kids choking, inserted into body |
| Electric X-mas decorations | 3,300 | "Griswald's Christmas Vacation" |
| Vending machines | 2,900 | Tipping over, hot coffee spilling out |
| Hammocks | 2,500 | The "Gilligan and the Skipper effect" |

*Source: U.S. Consumer Product Safety Commissions, 2001.*

## LONGEVITY AND THE REAL RETIREMENT RISK

The size of your Social Security check is only one piece of your early retirement puzzle. Another huge risk linked to your longevity lies in outliving your other retirement resources.

With that insight in mind, you are ready for the third question: are you married? As the Lifestyle and Family Longevity Questionnaire indicated, marriage has a positive effect on your life span. And when it comes to benefits, marriage is a big factor in determining if you want to retire early and receive benefits. If you are married, go back and determine your spouse's longevity with the tools provided and fill it in below as well.

## Is a Decision Possible?
No. Knowing your benefits, breakevens, and your estimate of longevity is not enough. You need more information.

Please write your benefit information from chapter 1 and longevity from this chapter below so you can build toward the right decision in the next chapters.

|  | Early Retire at 62 | Full Retire NRA | Late Retire at 70 |
|---|---|---|---|
| Benefits Amount |  |  |  |
| Break-even Ages |  |  |  |
| Personal Longevity Assessment |  |  |  |
| Spouse's Longevity Assessment |  |  |  |

# CHAPTER THREE

# Are You Married?

Approximately 73 percent of men over age 65 are married and living with their wives. Half of the women of the same age are living with their husbands according to the National Institute on Aging. These facts are very important because marriage can greatly affect your spouse's benefits if he or she collects on your earnings record.

The SSA has specific rules; just a marriage certificate will not do. Your spouse needs to be married to you for at least a year and the marriage must be legally valid in the state in which it is performed. As we will begin to see, whatever marriage you may have entered into or exited, Social Security has a rule to deal with it.

If the marriage has not lasted a year, but the wife bore the husband's child, then the year requirement is waived. Also if a marriage was performed in good faith, but becomes legally invalid because of a flaw in the marriage procedures or the ceremony, it is "deemed a valid marriage" by the Social Security Administration under some very specific conditions. Finally, if you are part of a common-law marriage, you must live in a state that recognizes such marriages.

## SPOUSAL BENEFITS AND PENALTIES

As early as age 62, spouses can collect either on their own career benefits, or take 50 percent of their spouses' benefits, whichever is greater. The non-working spouse can begin to collect on the other's record only if the working spouse has already begun receiving benefits, a small but very important point. If the non-working spouse is taking care of a child under the age of 16 or who is disabled, then those benefits can begin before the earliest retirement age of 62 under other circumstances.

But for the spouse of an early retiree collecting early retirement benefits, things get even more complicated. If the primary beneficiary takes early retirement, there is a modest reduction of benefits for the primary. But if the spouse elects early retirement, based on the primary beneficiary's record, there is a drastic reduction in benefits for the spouse. For example, what if my brother Richard, who was born in 1957, decides to retire at the age of 62. He will receive 72.5 percent of his full retirement benefit. His wife (and my sister-in-law) Doris, who is the same age as Richard, also wants to retire at age 62 and has elected to take her Social Security based on her husband's contributions to Social Security. Because her benefits will be based on his reduced early retirement benefits, she will receive only 33.75 percent of his potential full benefits, instead of 50 percent. That drastic reduction must be considered when doing financial planning.

If Doris decides to wait until she is 63 or 64, her benefits will increase. If she waits until her full retirement age of 66 and 6 months (remember the age is increasing past age 65), then her benefits will not be reduced beyond the standard 50 percent reduction that a spouse regularly collects of the primary beneficiary's benefits. If Richard had decided to continue working until he reached full retirement age, Doris could still retire at age 62, but she would have to collect on her own earnings record, or wait until Richard retires to begin collecting.

This difference in timing for couples is very common. According to a 2004 survey by the Center for Retirement Research at Boston College, 20 percent of couples retire in the same year and 50 percent retire within two years of each other. This timing can be due to differences in ages, preference, or the desire to continue the couple's health benefits from the continuing worker's employer until Medicare begins for both at age 65.

## EARLY RETIREMENT BENEFITS FOR SPOUSES

| Year of Birth | Full Retirement Age (NRA) | Age 62 Reduction Months | Spouse's Monthly % Reduction* | Spouse's Total Reduction at Age 62 | Spouse's Benefit as % of Full Benefits | Employed Spouse's Benefit as % of Full Benefits |
|---|---|---|---|---|---|---|
| 1942 | 65+10 m | 46 | 0.634 | 64.58 | 35.42 | 75.83 |
| 1943–1954 | 66 | 48 | 0.625 | 65.00 | 35.00 | 75.00 |
| 1955 | 66+2 m | 50 | 0.617 | 65.42 | 34.58 | 74.16 |
| 1956 | 66+4 m | 52 | 0.609 | 65.84 | 34.16 | 73.34 |
| **1957** | **66+6 m** | **54** | **0.602** | **66.25** | **33.75** | **72.50** |
| 1958 | 66+8 m | 56 | 0.595 | 66.67 | 33.33 | 71.67 |
| 1959 | 66+10 m | 58 | 0.589 | 67.08 | 32.92 | 70.83 |
| 1960+ | 67 | 60 | 0.583 | 67.50 | 32.50 | 70.00 |

* Does not include the 50% standard reduction that a spouse receives at NRA.

Source: SSA.

## SURVIVOR BENEFITS

What happens if the dependent spouse outlives the spouse whose earnings had determined the benefits? Let's assume Doris outlives Richard. If she is at least 60 years old and married to him for at least nine months before Richard dies, then she can collect a Survivor's Social Security check of 71.5 percent of Richard's benefits at age 60 up to 100 percent of

Richard's benefits at Doris's full retirement age. If Richard had decided on early retirement for himself, Doris will collect her percentage on his reduced benefits. If Doris were much younger than Richard, and he died while taking early Social Security retirement, her survivor benefits would be reduced for his early retirement for a much longer time for Doris's lifetime.

It is very important to note that *Doris does not obtain spousal survivor benefits in addition to her own.* One of the most misunderstood areas of Social Security is that a surviving spouse collects only one check, not two. You collect based upon which benefit is higher. Therefore if your Social Security income as a couple is vitally important to make ends meet, the death of a spouse could jeopardize the lifestyle of the survivor.

In an odd twist in the law that is often misunderstood, if Doris qualifies for retirement benefits on her own record and also as Richard's surviving spouse, she can elect to receive reduced early retirement benefits until her full retirement then switch to 100 percent of the survivor benefits based on Richard's work record without a penalty for receiving the early retirement benefits on her own record.

If Doris, the survivor, is over age 60 and marries a new husband Sam, she can collect on Richard's record if the benefits are higher than those based on her own record or Sam's record. Also, if Doris were taking care of a child under age 16 or who is disabled at the time of Richard's untimely demise, any extra reductions for early retirement are waived and she receives the working spouse's benefits.

## GOVERNMENT EMPLOYEES AND TEACHERS

There are over 20 million federal, state, and local government workers who do not pay anything into the Social Security system, including 3 million teachers. They do not pay FICA taxes on their wages to the Social Security system. Therefore, many couples reading this book may have at least one spouse working for the government or as a teacher under different retirement rules. These rules have enormous implications for your retirement income. The little black book for these special rules regarding Social Security for the spouse's benefits is found in the fine print of the Government Pension Offset. The SSA will deduct the government pension from the Social Security benefits that a spouse, widow, or widower might otherwise be entitled. If you became eligible for spousal benefits after July 1983, two-thirds of the government pension is offset against the Social Security benefits as a spouse or widow. If the spouse did not work at all, he or she would be entitled to more benefits.

"Why does the Social Security system have the offset?" It sounds unfair. The reason is that the system is based on universal participation of all earners to support all participating earners, their spouses, and their dependents, in their retirement. Government workers who did not contribute to the Social Security system are therefore not eligible for full benefits from the system to which they potentially could have made contributions.

A loophole existed that allowed teachers who never paid anything into Social Security during their career to qualify for full spousal benefits by working a single day before they retired. This was a very popular technique that teachers in Texas led the pack in taking advantage of. School districts aided their teachers by providing a day of work moving furniture or cleaning schools for wages subject to Social Security taxes. In many cases, the teachers paid the school districts to "hire" them for the day. Teachers, school bus drivers, cafeteria workers, university administrators, health science center employees, and counselors from fourteen states participated. Fortunately for the health of the Social Security system, that loophole was plugged in July 2004.

A rule that is similar to Government Offset for spouses, but instead directly affects the primary worker's benefits, is the Windfall Elimination Provision. If you were a federal worker hired before 1984, your benefits are reduced by up to $280.50 a month (in 2001 dollars), if you are eligible to collect both Social Security benefits for covered work and a federal pension. If you have a substantial working record covered by Social Security, this reduction may be minimal.

### Private Pension Plan Shockers

Many company pensions perform a "pension offset" in reverse, in what can be a very nasty surprise when you retire. Companies offset their company pension obligations against Social Security. Bob, a retired pharmaceutical sales executive I met on an airplane, told me his company reduced his pension, and he did not know it until he retired. These company pensions often call this sneaky offset "coordinating benefits" with your Social Security benefits. In this way they add your company pension and Social Security benefits together, use a formula to replace a certain percentage of your working income, and then determine your private pension benefits. If your Social Security benefits are high enough, then the company pension is able to pay you less, because the combination adds up to a preset percentage outlined buried in the company's plan documents. The company saves a great deal of money and enjoys your loyalty during your working years because you believe that your pension will come to you in full when you retire. These offset provisions are very common, and you should inquire about them before you receive a shock at retirement time.

## HAVE KIDS?

The accepted age of parenthood has increased over the years, not withstanding the late parenthood of the biblical Sarah and Abraham at the age of 90 or Anthony Quinn in his 80s. I have two children and I can't even imagine being a father to young children during my retirement, but about 10 percent of retirees are. It is very conceivable that you could have had children at the age of 43, or adopt children, and still have a dependent child 19 years old or younger when you retire early at age 62. If you do have dependents, they can collect from Social Security if you do.

Regardless of your need, a check is still a check. You can collect a Social Security check for unmarried, dependent children up to the age of 18. Children can be as old as 19 if they are also full-time students at an accredited school, attending twenty hours a week in at least a thirteen-week course, and not paid by an employer to attend the school. If you have a dependent, disabled child he or she can collect into adulthood.

Your grandchildren are eligible for benefits if their parents are deceased or totally disabled and the grandchildren are dependent on you. Under certain circumstances stepchildren, illegitimate children, and adopted children are eligible. They cannot collect these dependent checks unless you begin collecting benefits yourself. The amount of those checks depends on your earnings record and the number of dependents. Children are generally eligible for 50 percent of the worker's monthly benefits. There are family maximums that strictly limit the benefits derived from one worker's record so that large families cannot overburden the system.

## FAMILY MAXIMUM PAYMENTS

Suppose a retired male worker like Richard later in life marries a younger woman after Doris passes away, has a dozen kids, and lives in a shoe. Richard could live comfortably on six extra full checks (12 kids × 50 percent), quite a novel retirement plan—but not permitted. The limit on a family is approximately 1.5 to 2 times Richard's retirement monthly payment at full retirement (NRA) as determined by complex calculations performed by the SSA. The SSA calculates a Primary Insurance Amount (PIA) and that is what the family maximum payment is based on, even if the retiree takes early retirement. The "primary" earner's benefit is first subtracted from the family maximum. The remainder is then apportioned to the eligible dependants, including the spouse. A Claims Representative will make that exact calculation when you apply for benefits, so relax.

In a family with dependents there are often two working spouses. Two working spouses do not double the maximum family benefit. It is higher than just one working spouse, but somewhat less than double. Again this is an issue for your well-trained Claims Representative from the SSA to calculate.

## DIVORCED SPOUSES CAN COLLECT

Divorced spouses can collect as well. As divorces are complicated, so are the Social Security rules for divorced spouses. Couples must have been married for at least ten years and divorced for two years to be eligible. Suppose Doris and Richard divorce later in life. Doris, a non-working spouse, can collect on Richard's work record if she is at least 62 years old and has not remarried. She would collect the same amount a married spouse would: 50 percent of the ex-spouse's benefits at full retirement or less at age 62, or 100 percent as a survivor at her full retirement age. Richard also must be at least 62 years old and have enough credits to qualify for his own Social Security benefits. Their ten years of marriage must be continuous, not the sum of years of failed marriages and remarriages to each other. (Remember, the folks at Social Security have seen it all.) If you are a spouse thinking about divorce and are just shy of your tenth anniversary, stick it out for a few more months for your own good. If you are under 60 and qualify for your ex's survivor benefits, you forfeit them if you remarry and stay married.

Doris can collect benefits on Richard's record even if Richard has not elected to receive retirement benefits, or has had his benefits suspended for excess earnings. If Doris were still married to Richard, she could not collect on Richard's record until he retires.

Doris's benefits do not affect Richard's benefits, even if Richard has a wife and several exes out there cursing him. Social Security does not want the actions of a divorced spouse to affect the other, otherwise it would be drawn into family battles and lawsuits that it simply doesn't have time or resources to get involved in.

And like other happily married spouses, Doris can still opt for her own Social Security benefits based on her own earnings records, if that produces a greater benefit. If Doris marries again and wants to collect from new husband Sam's work record, she needs to be remarried for at least a year and be age 62.

The family maximum benefits that may constrain the benefits of a working spouse's dependents do not apply to their divorced spouse's potential benefits. In the eyes of the SSA, the divorced spouse is part of a "separate family unit." Again, if that were not the case, the SSA would get involved in ugly family disputes as the actions of a divorced spouse could dramatically affect the other's benefits. Imagine the fights that would occur when, with each additional birth of a child with a new wife, would come with a reduction of benefits for the divorced wife.

# DEPENDENT PARENTS CAN COLLECT

The Social Security system is very generous. If a worker dies and leaves dependent parents, they can collect a check. It is rare, but it happens. A surviving parent can collect if the working adult child was the source of half or more of his or her support. The parent must be at least age 62, not married since the child's death, and not entitled to a larger retirement check or disability check on his or her own. With those criteria met, the parent can collect 82 percent of the worker's full retirement benefits. If two dependent parents survive, each is separately entitled to 75 percent of their child's full retirement benefits as long as the other qualifications are met and family maximum limits are not exceeded. Complicated indeed.

At this point you have three pieces of the puzzle in place to make your early retirement decision. You have an idea what your benefits are; approximately how long you need to live to break even to collect the most benefits; and an idea of how long you might live to enjoy your checks.

## Is a Decision Possible?

No. Knowing your benefits, breakevens, longevity, and the effects of your decision on spousal and dependents' benefits is not enough. You need more information.

Please write down your benefits information from chapter 1, longevity information from chapter 2, and dependents information from this chapter below so that you can move on to the next chapter and build toward your decision.

| Spousal Benefits: | Early Retire at 62 | Full Retire NRA | Late Retire at 70 |
|---|---|---|---|
| Benefits Amount | | | |
| Break-even Ages | | | |
| Spouse's Longevity Estimate | | | |
| Other Dependants' Benefits | | | |

| Your Benefits (from the last chapter) | Early Retire at 62 | Full Retire NRA | Late Retire at 70 |
|---|---|---|---|
| Benefits Amount | | | |
| Break-even Ages | | | |
| Personal Longevity Assessment | | | |

# CHAPTER FOUR

# Planning on Working While "Retired"?

How working during retirement affects your benefits is one of the most misunderstood, and probably the most complicated, aspects of your early retirement decision process. It is a very important piece of the retirement picture, as Deborah Russell who develops workplace programs for the American Association for Retired Persons (AARP) says: "Baby Boomers will probably end up financing retirement with work." When AARP surveyed 1,200 Baby Boomers in 2003, almost eight in ten said that they expected to take a job after retiring.

| HOW MOST BOOMERS SAY THEY WILL WORK IN RETIREMENT | |
| --- | --- |
| Part time employment for enjoyment | 38% |
| Part time for income | 32% |
| Start a business | 19% |
| Full time at a new job | 9% |
| Other | 2% |

*Source: AARP, Walter Updegrave, Real World Retirement Guide, Money, 11/04, p.98.*

Every year, more and more people continue to work past their traditional retirement age. Continuing to work keeps you mentally active, productive, and useful. The real question is whether you will choose to pursue it full time or part time, as paid or volunteer work.

If you continue to earn income and take early retirement benefits, you may face unpleasant consequences. First, the SSA can reduce your benefits if you earn over a certain level. Second, the IRS may tax the benefits received once you have them. When I read the guidelines from these government agencies, I noticed that neither agency referenced the other. So if you read only the SSA guidelines, you think you have a comprehensive answer when in reality you have only half the answer. Understandable as they both are giving a full answer on how working during retirement affects *their* calculations, you need to look at the whole picture.

It is surprising that authoritative sources do not adequately address the issue of working while retired. It can make a huge difference, as our example with Nancy has shown. She would lose 62 percent of her early retirement benefits by choosing to work. Experts have created elaborate quantitative analyses with charts and graphs on the issue of retiring early, but often ignore the consequences of continuing to work. In the July 2004 issue of the *Journal of Financial Planning* there is an elaborate eight-page analysis of the early retirement issue. It concluded, "The differences in the economic values do not appear to be significant enough in *any* of the situations to be a major factor influencing the decision as to when to begin Social Security." In their defense it does say, "many factors should be considered before making the decision to retire." However, financial planners who read the magazine are left with the impression that collecting Social Security early is not an issue.

A cover story of *USA Today* on January 25, 2005, about retiring and collecting early Social Security benefits proclaimed,

"In the long run, it comes out even." "On average it doesn't matter." The writer considered many factors including longevity, spousal benefits, and a short work history, but working during early retirement was not one of them. "Bottom line: Retire from [age] 62 through 69 and you have little to gain or lose." Of course, if you are like Nancy, giving up 62 percent of your benefits, you have plenty to lose.

In the *AARP Bulletin Online* in November 2002, a similar incorrect assertion is made. "I always suggest that people take the benefit early because the break-even-point is after 80," says Bryan Place, a financial planner in Manlius, NY. "Using even a fairly conservative rate of return, early retirement gives you a higher value," says Clarence Rose, professor of finance at Radford University.

In the *Journal of Retirement Planning* of July-August 2002, Mimi Lord summarized the TIAA-CREF Institute's sixteen-page study by Thomas Walsh. "If you or your clients have been agonizing about whether to start Social Security benefits early or to wait until normal retirement age, the good news is that you can relax. For most people, the present value of the financial benefits they would receive under either scenario is very similar, meaning that other factors such as health or cash needs often play a bigger role in the decision. So while you probably won't go seriously wrong with either decision, there are some guiding factors that can help improve your decision-making process."

I wouldn't relax, nor would I suggest that Nancy or you relax. The issue of earning while collecting benefits is central to your planning for Social Security. Quite honestly, when I began to do my research for this book, I was misled by these articles at first, but I soon found out that working while retired can be *the* most important factor in your early benefits decision.

One of the few sources that did correctly address the working issue was The Motley Fool Web site in March 2000. David

Braze wrote, "I intend to wait because I have sufficient wage income to cause me to lose all of an age-62 benefit anyway, and I enjoy what I do." The Motley Fool was no fool on this issue!

## THE SOCIAL SECURITY SYSTEM AND PENALIZING WORK

The SSA penalizes early retirees who continue to work and earn over $12,000 [2005] in their first years of early retirement beginning at age 62 until their last calendar year in which they reach their full retirement age. The SSA adjusts this limit upward annually for inflation. In some cases, even the income that you earned before you turn age 62 reduces your benefits. Benefits are reduced by $1 for every $2 of earnings over the $12,000 earnings limit. If you earn more than the monthly prorated amount of $1,000 ($12,000 divided by 12) a month during the first calendar year of your early retirement, you are penalized. The SSA calls this process its Annual Earnings Test.

In the final calendar year in which you reach your full retirement age, the system allows you more earnings without a penalty. For income over $31,800 [2005], the SSA reduces benefits by only $1 for every $3 over the higher limit. Both limits are annually indexed upward for inflation. Fortunately, once you reach your full retirement age, the government no longer penalizes or limits your earnings, thanks to the Senior Citizens' Freedom to Work Act of 2000 signed into law by President Clinton. This provides seniors a strong disincentive to work during early retirement, or a strong incentive to delay retirement if they are working.

If you choose to earn money during your early retirement years, those wages will be added to your earnings record and increase your overall benefits going forward. If you had years with zero earnings in the record of your 35 highest earning years on which your benefits are computed, the added earnings can be very beneficial. Your retirement benefits will be recomputed automatically to take into account the updated earnings record. Your benefits will be increased accordingly for all your checks going forward.

The lists below will clarify what the SSA determines to be earned income for its Annual Earnings Test.

### *Income included in the Annual Earnings Test calculation (earned income)*

- Gross wages from employment, even if not subject to Social Security taxes
- Profit-sharing payments from an employer
- Bonuses and awards earned during retirement
- Advances against future earnings as an employee
- Sick and vacation pay earned during retirement
- "Subject to call" earnings
- Net earnings from self-employment, net of any loss from self-employment when received (or when "accrued" if the accrual method is used), regardless of when the services were actually performed. If earned before retirement, it must be proved to the SSA.
- Royalties from a copyright or patent obtained during early retirement

### *Income not included in the Annual Earnings Test (passive income)*

- Interest
- Dividends
- Capital gains
- IRA distributions
- Damage awards
- Income from a hobby if not significant
- Prizes and awards

- Inheritance
- Rental income
- Pensions
- Severance pay related to pre-retirement work
- Royalties from patents or copyrights from personally created works created before retirement [The royalties from my first book, *The Ten-Day MBA*, would not count against me.]
- Wages, bonuses, severance, sick pay, and vacation pay received during retirement but attributable to employment before retirement, *but* you need to tell the SSA about it when you apply and prove it to the SSA; otherwise the SSA will attribute it to the year when received. The SSA refers to any income received during retirement from your former employer for work done prior to retirement as Special Wage Payments (SWP).
- Unemployment benefits
- Workers' compensation payments

The SSA says that the theory behind including only earned income for the Earnings Test is that, "the Social Security retirement program insures against loss of earnings from work and not against the failure to have investment income." It does not tax such earnings and therefore does not penalize for them.

## What Does that Mean for You?

If you are still working during retirement and earning a substantial income (like our example of Nancy at the beginning of the book), your benefits are slashed. In her case her plans to work cut her benefits by 62 percent. At that point the whole issue of break-even age is insignificant in comparison. The issue of investing your benefits is a moot point as well. Accepting the greatly reduced early retirement benefit versus receiving a full retirement benefit without the deductions would not make sense because the payback for waiting would be so short. Also, if you earn near or under the limits then this will not be an issue for you. However, as shown in Nancy's case, her modest $25,000 salary working part-time during early retirement would practically wipe out her Social Security check.

In cases that you retire early and really need to use all your benefits and need to earn as well, the permanent reductions in benefits for early retirement, not reductions for earnings, can drastically affect your lifestyle throughout your retirement. It is a choice that needs to be weighed carefully.

## Look Out If You Are Self-Employed

Self-employed people have some extra hoops to pass through for their benefits evaluation. Approximately 10 percent of workers over 50 are self-employed. "Among workers age 51 to 69 who are self-employed, fully one-third made the jump after turning 50" according to the AARP and the Rand Corp. The SSA is savvy that self-employed people have more latitude in determining their salary and income than employed people. As Robert Kiyosaki's best seller *Rich Dad, Poor Dad* describes, self-employed people can easily convert their personal expenses into company expenses and can influence in which year income is realized.

Knowing that a self-employed person can determine his or her own salary, the SSA will view your entire year's salary and assume you are over the earnings limit, even if you reduce your salary after early retirement begins. You will need to prove to the SSA that your duties have been substantially reduced to justify the reduced salary. If your business continues, the SSA will ask who assumed your duties and what their qualifications are. The SSA will require your personal and corporate tax returns to ensure that business activity is not hidden by including earnings on one return and not the other. Also, the SSA will view any deductions used to take money from your business, but not used to formally pay your salary, with suspicion. The SSA will require a signed personal statement detailing the business activity, your duties, and how they were reduced in retirement. You will be asked to include information on how your hours have changed, what compensation and other payments you have received, and who your major customers and suppliers are, so the SSA can verify your story. It also makes the job of lying much harder, and easier for criminal prosecution should you falsely claim benefits. Your lie would be in black and white and not subject to the foggy memories of conversations with a SSA representative. The SSA has experienced all types of scam artists and its representatives have heard all the stories. Penalties for fraud can range from a fine of $500 to $10,000 and/or imprisonment of one to fifteen years.

Another ploy used to deceive the SSA is selling your business to a relative, yet continuing to operate the business and receiving compensation off the record. If you sell your business, you must produce a real contract of sale that shows that the business was transferred for a reasonable price to a third party. Deceptive tactics don't work; honesty is the best policy.

You can be honest and make the most from the system if you and your spouse run a family business. Married couples working together have the chance to allocate salary between them in ways that can maximize their Social Security benefits. Say my brother Richard and his wife Doris ran a bike shop. By knowing how the SSA calculates each person's benefits, it is possible that Richard may want to allocate more to his salary to maximize their cumulative family benefits. Because a spouse is able to collect 50 percent of the benefits of the larger of the spousal wage earners at full retirement, it may be more advantageous to load more of the earnings into his earnings record, the record on which the SSA calculates his primary benefits and hence her spousal benefits. As long as the allocation is reasonable and is based on actual contributions made to the family business, you can do it. By creating the largest earnings records on which both spouses' benefits are based can make a big difference calculating your initial benefits. If the total income for the business is greater than the individual maximum income subject to Social Security taxes, it will cost more in current Social Security taxes but will provide increased benefits in the long run. In any case, this ploy requires careful review of the Social Security rules and cost/benefit calculations to ensure that it is the best course for you.

## REPORTING EARNINGS DURING EARLY RETIREMENT

When you file for benefits, your Claims Representative will ask you to estimate what you will earn during your first retirement year. Your benefits will be adjusted accordingly as explained in the section about the Annual Earnings Test. If you start to receive benefits in the last three months of the calendar year, you will be asked to estimate the next year's earnings as well.

The SSA also collects information from your W-2 forms and self-employment tax payments thereafter to calculate your payments. You may be asked to report your earnings as well if you have substantial self-employment income or income that varies widely from month to month. If you are asked by the SSA, you are required to submit an Annual Report of Earnings and a report of an estimate for the next year's earnings. The SSA will adjust your benefits accordingly and deduct the amount from the monthly benefits based on the actual W-2 information it receives the next year. If you know of any significant changes, you need to notify the SSA as soon as possible, not after the change occurs. That prevents overpayments and underpayments from occurring. If there are overpayments to you, the SSA will deduct them from your future check or checks, unless you petition that the overpayments all be taken out evenly over the next year's checks.

If the SSA asks for an annual report or estimate, you must file no later than April 15th following the year. The SSA will send you the form. There are penalties for not filing a report for the years in which you were overpaid benefits. The penalties and the overpayments are taken from your future benefits payments until they are fully paid back to the SSA.

If your excess earnings resulting from the Annual Earnings Test wipe out your early retirement benefits after you start receiving them, the SSA will stop your benefits. When you earn less, and are entitled to some benefits greater than $0, your early retirement benefits will resume. The months in which you do not any receive benefits will not penalize your full retirement benefits. But you need to be proactive about it, because the penalties for early retirement are steep and permanent. If your benefits are cut drastically to a nominal amount because of new income during early retirement, you should consider halting benefits quickly, before they actually become $0. Don't be lazy about this one, because a few dollars per month in early retirement benefits (anything over $0) will cost you thousands in full retirement benefits. The SSA's stiff early retirement penalties apply to your benefits throughout your retirement whether you collected a dollar or a thousand dollars a month during your early retirement.

## THE IRS TAXES YOUR BENEFITS

The IRS and the SSA exist in entirely different universes. They work independently to determine their attacks on your check. The SSA adjusts your benefits before the check goes out. The

IRS taxes your benefits when you file your tax return, after the year is over. The IRS taxes Social Security benefits as long as you receive benefits in early and full retirement. The IRS throws a wider net than the SSA in its calculations and includes most forms of earned, *and* passive income that the SSA does not count for its Annual Earnings Test. The SSA uses the Annual Earnings Test only during early retirement and does not penalize your benefits afterward. In the retirement planning information provided by the SSA, there is very little attention paid to the IRS's taxation of benefits.

To determine the potential tax on your benefits, you first figure out your Base Amount. You add one half of the benefits you received, and all your earnings as shown on your tax form as the Aggregate Gross Income, plus any tax-exempt interest. If the Base Amount exceeds $25,000 for a single person or $32,000 for a married couple, then 50 percent of the benefits are taxable. If you file a joint return with a spouse, both of your incomes must be included in the Base Amount calculation, even if one of the spouses does not receive benefits.

For so-called "upper income" seniors with a Base Amount above $34,000 for a single person or $44,000 for a couple, 85 percent of benefits are taxed, not 50 percent. I don't know about you, but I do not consider $44,000 a wealthy couple's income. If you and your spouse are married and living together but file as "married filing separately," 85 percent of your benefits are taxable without regard to a Base Amount.

These income taxes on your Social Security benefits were earmarked to fund Medicare when enacted, not to support retirement benefits. This bold move was passed under the leadership of President Clinton in 1993 in his first term to help plug the projected shortfall in Medicare.

IRS Publications 554 and 915 fully describes the rules. In IRS Publication 915 there is a worksheet that guides you through the exact calculation when you do your income taxes. It may seem complicated but the numbers are taken straight from your tax return as follows:

| CALCULATION OF FEDERAL INCOME TAX ON SOCIAL SECURITY BENEFITS | |
|---|---|
| Total Social Security Benefits from your SS-1099(s) | $_____ |
| Enter ½ of Benefits | $_____ |
| Total of Income (total of both spouses if applicable) | |
| Wages | _____ |
| Interest including Tax Exempt Interest | _____ |
| Dividends | _____ |
| Alimony | _____ |
| Business Income (Schedule C) | _____ |
| Capital Gains (Schedule D) | _____ |
| Taxable IRA Distributions | _____ |
| Taxable Pension Distributions | _____ |
| Rental, Royalty and Partnership, Sub S. Corp Income | _____ |
| Farm Income | _____ |
| Unemployment Compensation | _____ |
| Other Income | _____ |
| US Savings Bond Interest | _____ |
| Total Income | $_____ |
| Add ½ Benefits and Total Income | $_____ |
| This is your "Base Amount" | $_____ |

FILING STATUS:

*Single, Head of Household, Qualifying Widow(er) or Married Filing Separately While Living Apart*

| Base Amount of $25,000 to $34,000 | 50% of Benefits Taxable |
| Base Amount of more than $34,000 | 85% of Benefits Taxable |

*Married Filing Jointly*

| Base Amount $32,000 to $44,000 | 50% of Benefits Taxable |
| Base Amount over $44,000 | 85% of Benefits Taxable |

*Married Filing Separately While Living Together*
*Regardless of Income*                                85% of Benefits Taxable
Social Security Benefits                              $_____
Select Taxable percent based on Filing Status
   and Base Amount total                        × _____ %
                                                     (0, 50%, 85%)
Multiply By Your Tax Rate                            × _____ %
In 2005:
   10% for Taxable Incomes not over $7,300
   15% for Taxable Incomes $7,300 to $29,700
   25% for Taxable Incomes $29,700 to $71,950
   28% for Taxable Incomes $71,950 to $150,150
   33% for Taxable Incomes of $150,150 to $319,100
   35% for Taxable Incomes over $319,100

*Tax on Social Security Benefits*                    $_____

   Source: IRS Form 915.

Nancy, our everyday working woman, would owe $646 to the IRS from her $5,068 in Social Security benefits. Because taxes are not taken out of your benefits check as they are from a paycheck many Social Security recipients find the tax on their benefits an unpleasant surprise the following year.

Nancy has $5,068 in benefits, $25,000 of regular earnings, $2,300 profit from renting her duplex, and $8,600 from dividends and interest on her portfolio. Unfortunately, her Base Amount totals to $38,434, which is higher than the special IRS provision for "upper income" seniors. For seniors earning above $34,000 as a single person or $44,000 for a couple, 85 percent of their benefits are taxed, not just 50 percent. Using a 15 percent tax rate applied to 85 percent of her benefits, Nancy's remaining benefits are reduced by a tax of $646 to $4,422.

## CALCULATION OF FEDERAL INCOME TAX ON NANCY'S PROJECTED BENEFITS

| | |
|---|---|
| Total Social Security Benefits | $5,068 |
| ½ of Benefits (the use of ½ here in the calculation is independent of the percentage of benefits that are ultimately considered taxable, 50% or 85%) | $2,534 |
| Total Income | |
| Wages | $25,000 |
| Interest and Dividends | $8,600 |
| Rental profits | $2,300 |
| Total Income | $35,900 |
| Add ½ SS Benefits | $2,534 |
| Total Base Amount | $38,434 |
| Nancy's Social Security Benefits | $5,068 |
| Select Taxable percent based on Filing Single and Base Amount total if > $34,000 | × 85% |
| Multiply By Your Tax Rate* | × 15% |
| Tax on Nancy's Benefits | $646 |

*$35,900 income − $4,750 standard deduction − $3,050 personal exemption = $28,100 net taxable income that is subject to a 15% rate in 2005.

The $11,568 of total benefit that Nancy was expecting to receive as her early retirement reward has now withered by 62 percent to $4,422 after reductions and taxes. Ouch! Working and earning during retirement can be the most significant factor in your Social Security equation.

# Is a Decision Possible?

No. Knowing your benefits, breakevens, longevity, effects of your decision on spousal and dependents' benefits, penalties for working, and income taxes on your benefits is not enough.
You need more information.

What you need during retirement and what your other resources are may influence your calculations so it is a bit premature to make your final early retirement decision. At this stage you should find out and write down what you, your spouse, and eligible dependents potentially will be receiving in full Social Security benefits, your longevity estimates and breakeven years which you should have gathered in the first three chapters.

Then you need to estimate what you both plan to earn during early retirement and reduce your full retirement benefits by the applicable Annual Earnings Test penalties and federal income taxes using the rules and worksheet provided in this chapter. You may want to refer to your current tax returns for income data and make adjustments for changes during your retirement.

| Your Projectal Net Benefits Calculation | Early Retire at 62 | Full Retire NRA | Late Retire 70 |
|---|---|---|---|
| Benefits Projected (chapter 1) | | | |
| Less Annual Earnings Test Reductions (this chapter) | | | |
| Less Federal Income Taxes (this chapter) | | | |
| = Net Projected Benefits | | | |
| Break-even Ages (chapter 1) | | | |
| Longevity Estimate (chapter 2) | | | |

*continued*

| Your Spouse's Net Benefits Calculation | Early Retire at 62 | Full Retire NRA | Late Retire at 70 |
|---|---|---|---|
| Benefits Projected (chapter 1) | | | |
| Less Annual Earnings Test Reductions* (this chapter) | | -0- | -0- |
| Less Federal Income Taxes (this chapter) | | | |
| = Net Projected Benefits | | | |
| Break-even Ages (chapter 1) | | | |
| Spouse's Longevity Estimate (chapter 2) | | | |

| Your Eligible Dependents' Benefits Calculation | Early Retire at 62 | Full Retire NRA | Late Retire at 70 |
|---|---|---|---|
| Benefits Projected (chapter 3) | | | |
| Less Annual Earnings Test Reductions* (this chapter) | | -0- | -0- |
| = Net Projected Benefits | | | |

*\* Caused by the earnings of the primary worker on which the benefits are based.*

# CHAPTER FIVE

# What Are Your Cash Needs During Retirement?

Retirement means different things to people. Some see it an opportunity to spend more time with family and friends. Others view this as the time to pursue a hobby or get more involved with the community. It can be well-deserved freedom after a lifetime of work or be filled with limitations and frustration. Regardless of your plans, your future requires careful financial planning.

This chapter on retirement needs comes before my chapter about retirement savings because I do not want the savings evaluation to cloud your objectivity of your real needs. By completing this chapter you will be ahead of 50 percent of workers who do not even make the attempt to estimate their retirement needs.

Americans' record at saving is pretty poor, but I think they are in denial. The Employee Benefit Research Institute (EBRI) conducted a survey in 2003 and found that less than 25 percent of people ages 40 to 59 have saved $100,000 or more. Yet roughly two thirds say they are "somewhat" or "very" confident of having enough for retirement. This survey shows the disconnect between perception and reality: the amount of money people will need in retirement and how much they are saving are out of balance. It should be no surprise that nearly two thirds of those surveyed have never tried to calculate how much they need to save for retirement.

The following is a basic chart that groups your monthly expenses by category. Take a look at your present expenses and estimate what they would be during retirement for the lifestyle that you are planning. There are three columns, one for basic living expenses, one for discretionary expenses, and a total of the two. This is way to get a handle on the basic needs that must be covered by your income. Since your income is probably going to decline during retirement, it is critical to make this assessment. Fortunately, for most retirees many of life's big expenses are behind you, such as a mortgage and college educations for your kids. When you retire, you may have fewer lunches away from home and fewer expenses for dry cleaning, work clothing, and transportation.

So take the first step in assessing your cash needs during retirement by reviewing your shoebox filled with your recent year's receipts and make adjustments for the changes you forecast into retirement.

## YOUR ESTIMATE OF RETIREMENT NEEDS

| Monthly Expenses | Basic | Discretionary | Total |
|---|---|---|---|
| *HOUSING:* | | | |
| Rent or mortgage | _____ | _____ | _____ |
| Insurance (total/12) | _____ | _____ | _____ |
| Maintenance, repairs | _____ | _____ | _____ |
| Association fees | _____ | _____ | _____ |
| Utilities | _____ | _____ | _____ |
| Property/school taxes (total/12) | _____ | _____ | _____ |

| Monthly Expenses | Basic | Discretionary | Total |
|---|---|---|---|
| GROCERIES | ____ | ____ | ____ |
| TRANSPORTATION: | | | |
|    Car payment | ____ | ____ | ____ |
|    Insurance (total/12) | ____ | ____ | ____ |
|    Fuel | ____ | ____ | ____ |
|    Maintenance, repairs | ____ | ____ | ____ |
|    Registration/taxes (total/12) | ____ | ____ | ____ |
| HEALTH COSTS: | | | |
|    Health insurance premiums | ____ | ____ | ____ |
|    Medicare/Medigap | ____ | ____ | ____ |
|    Drugs not covered | ____ | ____ | ____ |
|    Co-pays | ____ | ____ | ____ |
|    Toiletries | ____ | ____ | ____ |
| PERSONAL INSURANCE PREMIUMS: | | | |
|    Life insurance (total/12) | ____ | ____ | ____ |
|    Long term care | ____ | ____ | ____ |
| ENTERTAINMENT: | | | |
|    Dining out | ____ | ____ | ____ |
|    Cable TV or satellite TV or radio | ____ | ____ | ____ |
|    Vacations (total/12) | ____ | ____ | ____ |
|    Internet access | ____ | ____ | ____ |
|    Movies and concerts | ____ | ____ | ____ |
|    Sporting fees/health club | ____ | ____ | ____ |
|    Books/magazines/paper | ____ | ____ | ____ |
|    Hobbies | ____ | ____ | ____ |
|    Other entertainment | ____ | ____ | ____ |
| CLOTHING | ____ | ____ | ____ |
| INCOME TAXES (TOTAL/12) | ____ | ____ | ____ |

*continued*

| Monthly Expenses (continued) | Basic | Discretionary | Total |
|---|---|---|---|
| CHARITABLE DONATIONS | ___ | ___ | ___ |
| GIFTS AND PRESENTS | ___ | ___ | ___ |
| CREDIT CARD DEBT PAYMENTS | ___ | ___ | ___ |
| BANK CHARGES | ___ | ___ | ___ |
| LEGAL AND ACCOUNTING | ___ | ___ | ___ |
| OFFICE SUPPLIES | ___ | ___ | ___ |
| OTHER | ___ | ___ | ___ |
| **Total Monthly Expenses** | ___ | ___ | ___ |

There are more detailed worksheets available in the Retirement Planning section at *www.vanguard.com* that may help you create an even more accurate plan, but the one provided here is a great start. Vanguard's site is easy to use and has a highly rated family of low-cost mutual funds.

## Comments on Expense Areas

### Housing

If you are carrying a mortgage during your retirement the traditional mortgage deduction probably will be less valuable because either you are in a lower tax bracket, or you're simply using the standard deduction. If you are in the later years of your mortgage, most of your payment is repayment of principal and not deductible. Check if you are still paying a monthly fee for Private Mortgage Insurance (PMI). If you placed less than a 20 percent down payment on your house when you bought it you agreed to pay PMI. As your equity grows past 20 percent,

PMI becomes unnecessary, but you keep paying it until you cry "Uncle" and stop it.

Since you'll be spending more time at home, you may pay more attention to the condition of your home. Redecorating, new furniture, and home improvement that seemed unnecessary while you were working seem much more attractive when you are retired. Be careful not to create a money pit.

You may consider downsizing to a smaller home to save on real estate taxes, repairs, and other non-recurring expenses, but there are tax implications and costs to consider before selling your residence. In 2002 the tax rules changed from a one-time exclusion for seniors to exemptions that anyone can take. If you sell your main residence which you have owned and lived in for two years out of the five years prior to the sale, you can exclude $250,000 of the gain if you are single and $500,000 if a married couple filing jointly. This exclusion can be taken repeatedly, but you cannot exclude gains on another home sale within two years of taking this exemption. If you wanted to be daring, you could start an almost tax-free business becoming a serial home buyer by chasing houses that you think will rapidly appreciate in value because of the location or due to your own efforts to spruce it up. There are exceptions for the two year use rule for "unforeseen circumstances" such as death, divorce, and change of employment.

Before downsizing, see if your home can generate income. You may consider renting a room to a college student or another senior or offering your garage or basement as storage.

A study by the Bureau of Labor Statistics found that people over 65 years old spend more on health care and less on automobiles but, surprisingly, about the same on housing.

| SENIORS SPEND ABOUT THE SAME ON HOUSING AS EVERYONE ELSE | | |
|---|---|---|
| | **Ages 65+** | **All Households** |
| Health Care | 12.8% | 5.8% |
| Car Purchases | 6.5% | 9.0% |
| Housing | 32.6% | 32.7% |

Source: Bureau of Labor Statistics.

## Alternative Living Arrangements

Instead of living on your own, there are alternative living situations called Continuing Care Retirement Communities (CCRCs) that provide housing and continuing health care for healthy and independent retirees. In this setting housing and health and nursing care are guaranteed. One of the largest providers in my area is the non-profit company ACTS Retirement-Life Communities. They have been around for thirty years and have seventeen locations in the eastern United States (www.acts-retirement.org). For a substantial upfront payment, approximately $100,000, you "purchase" an apartment, and pay a monthly fee of approximately $1,000. The upfront payment is not refundable when you die as it pays for your care. You live in your own apartment with the freedom to go and come as you please, you are provided daily meals and the guarantee that as you need more care, you will be able to receive increasing levels of assistance, from in-apartment health services to full nursing-home care. The monthly fee does not change with your increasing need for care for ACTS facilities, but other assisted living situations often do escalate fees for increased levels of care. In these arrangements you may independently live out your life in your apartment or, if needed, you can transfer to more skilled care. These are very attractive packages that combine the positive aspects of long-term care insurance and comfortable housing. My wife's grandmother as well as my editor's mother had a very good experience with this type arrangement. However, if you choose this option, you need to maintain an adequate nest egg in the unlikely event the CCRC gets into financial trouble and is forced to raise its fees above those contracted for when you enter.

### Transportation

Review the insurance coverage for your car. When you retire you stop commuting to work, which should lower the miles you drive each week. Your insurance may reclassify your car as a "pleasure vehicle" and reduce your rates. You may also want to increase your deductible, which will reduce your premiums, but only if you have reduced the risk of an accident by not commuting. Be careful what you say to your agent, because a "retirement discount" is no discount at all; it's an increase! Some insurance companies assume retirees drive more, not less, during retirement, so don't ask for a retirement discount because you may end up with a "retirement penalty."

The make of car you own could make a big difference in your maintenance costs. The latest Powers studies show that Toyota and Honda have the best maintenance records and, not coincidentally, the Blue Book shows that they hold their value most over time.

When to buy a new car is another retirement issue. Do you trade in your car every few years or run it into the ground? For safety reasons I don't recommend keeping a decrepit car, but having a car payment on a constant basis isn't a good thing either. The best option is the invisible option of no car payment. If you choose a reliable car, you can drive it longer, have fewer repairs, and enjoy longer periods without monthly car payments.

### Health Insurance

If you retire early you probably will give up your employer's health insurance, unless your employer has a plan available until you are eligible for Medicare begins at age 65. Many who retire with health benefits may find that their former employers have reduced their benefits to save money. If a working spouse who turns 65 and goes on Medicare has a younger, non-working spouse on his or her employer's health plan, that spouse may be left without insurance. However, under COBRA you can pay to maintain the insurance you had while employed, for a period of eighteen months. You will pay whatever amount you paid while employed, plus your employer's share. If your company is generous it will allow you to remain on its plan until age 65.

Independently paying for your own health insurance can cost from $400 to $800 a month for a single person and $800 to $1200 for a couple. The rate is determined by your health and pre-existing conditions. If you have serious health issues you may not be able to get coverage. Unlike your employer-provided insurance where the lower cost of insuring healthy people balances the cost of insuring the sick, insurance companies evaluate individuals based on their individual medical histories. For some the insurance premiums are unaffordable, and that is why 18 percent of those approaching the full retirement age go without coverage.

Groups such as AARP offer plans for Medigap insurance after age 65, but not health insurance for early retirees and their families. AARP has begun a pilot program for early retirees with United Health Care, but it is not available in all states. Even in this pilot program, some applicants are rejected because they are too high a risk. Other than this pilot program, you are pretty much on your own. The cost can be more reasonable if you select a higher deductible of $1,000, $2,500, or more, and higher co-pays. In many instances, a higher deductible is better than paying a higher monthly payment. The same logic can be applied for your auto insurance deductible, too. Regardless of your deductible, health insurance costs have been escalating at a double-digit growth rate and have shown no signs of slowing down.

If you are working during early retirement and are under 65, there are health savings accounts (HSAs) that you may qualify for. They allow you to put aside pre-tax money like a 401(k) and use the money only for health expenditures. Unlike flexible-spending accounts provided by some employers to pay for health care expenses, HSAs allow unspent money to be rolled over from one year to the next. As reported in *Kiplinger's Personal Finance Magazine* in November 2004, these new plans are designed to help people who have high insurance deductibles and expenses. Your health insurance deductible has to be a minimum of $1,000 for a single person or $2,000 for a family, and it must be your only health insurance policy. From your HSA you can pay for your deductible, any co-pays, over-the-counter drugs, dental bills, vision costs, and even the cost of long term care insurance.

The government does not tax the money you invest in your HSA. It grows tax deferred and is not taxed when you withdraw money if it is used for medical expenses. You can use *www.ehealthinsurance.com* to estimate your benefits and *www.hsainsider.com* to find a plan if your employer does not offer one or if you are self-employed.

Under current law, as a retiree 55 years of age and older you can contribute up to the amount of your deductible plus $500 to a maximum of $2,600 for singles and $5,150 for a family. HSAs are a relatively new thing and many employers are starting to add them to their menu of benefits for their employees. If your income is substantial, your may qualify for significant tax savings; if not, the tax benefits may be minimal. You can deduct the contribution from your tax return even if you do not itemize deductions. So in the lowest tax bracket, a $1,000 contribution to your HSA would save you $100 in federal taxes.

### Personal Insurances

Life insurance is still a good idea for retirees if you have a spouse or dependents. If not, it makes no sense to begin an expensive insurance at this point in your life. Don't be deceived by inexpensive life insurance premiums for minimal coverage from TV advertisements and junk mail from aged talk show co-hosts.

Long term care insurance is very expensive, and a complicated purchase. The risk that you are insuring against is cost of a nursing home stay. A stay averages two and one-half years and $60,000 a year, less the cost paid by Medicare. According to John Willis (the long term care ombudsman for the state of Texas) in the *Wall Street Journal* in August 12, 2004, "Long-term care policy options and terms have become increasingly complex and restrictive, to the point that consumers often have no idea what it is they're buying." It's easy to get dizzy reading the policies and trying to understand the inclusions, exclusions, and limits of their coverage.

Coverage is increasingly more expensive because fewer companies, mainly due to corporate mergers, are offering it. Manulife Financial purchased John Hancock. Conseco went into bankruptcy. Aegon exited the long term care insurance business by selling its subsidiaries Transamerica Occidental Life, Life Investors Insurance, and Monumental Life. The majority of the business is controlled by three insurers: Manulife, MetLife, and General Electric's spin-off Genworth Financial. Another factor that causes increases in premiums is the poor rate of return on the investments made by the insurance companies with the premiums you pay. Longer lives of people receiving care and a lower lapse rate of people dropping their coverage before they receive any benefits also contribute to the high cost.

The critical option for coverage is the amount per day of benefits. Coverage can range from $50 to $500 per day. Some policies have inflation-protected benefits; others do not. Some require that you have a hospital stay before you are covered. Others have a waiting period of 30 to 90 days before coverage begins. Also, the facilities for your care may be defined in the policy in such a way that the type of facility or the home-care option you want may be excluded.

A study by *Consumer Reports* on long term care insurance in October 2003 found that policies are "too risky and too expensive" for most people. The magazine said that people who have household assets above $1.5 million (who can self-insure), or under $200,000 (who are covered by government programs), generally don't need long term care insurance. (The *Consumer Reports* study was originally misquoted by the *Wall Street Journal* as $20,000, not $200,000.) In addition, there is no guarantee the long term care insurer will be around in 20, 30, or 40 years, "when you need them to pay," the magazine says.

You may need to seek professional help in selecting your policy if you believe you need one. Even the most financially sophisticated individuals are confused with the complexity and the choices. There are so many ways for a policy to be constructed, it is nearly impossible to compare them.

Check out the insurers with the rating services that measure companies' financial strength, such as A.M. Best. If you are already near retirement age the premiums may be prohibitively expensive, or prohibitively restrictive due to your current state of health. So long term insurance may not even be an option for you.

During your working years you may have wisely purchased disability insurance. However, during retirement disability insurance that you carry may be of little use. Disability is defined differently by every policy. So it may mean that being retired precludes you from collecting any benefits by the definitions of your policy.

### Entertainment Expenses

This area is the most underestimated by retirees. The reality is that you will spend significantly more for entertainment during retirement, because you have time for having fun . . . and spending. The honeymoon stage of retirement, the time when you'll be most enjoying your new freedom, will be fade in several years, but the spending during the first years of retirement can create substantial bills. Review your entertainment expenses for the year before you retire, then increase it by 30 percent.

### Credit Card Debt Payments

If you are carrying large credit card balances and paying large amounts of monthly interest charges, it is imperative that you tackle this drain on your income. Often just a call to the credit card company, threatening to move your balance, will get a reduction in interest rate. (Find out the rates of the competition before you call.) Try it multiple times with different operators if it does not work the first time. If that eventually fails, roll over your balance to the cards you investigated. You can also take advantage of low introductory rates for moving your balance over to another card, but be ready to switch again before the full rate takes effect. In addition, you may want to convert all the high-interest debt into a lower cost home equity loan. If you are not getting desirable benefits from your credit card, consider applying for the Discover Card or AARP's Rewards Platinum Visa that pays "cash back" that you can use to pay part of your bill.

There are also some financial experts, such as Dave Ramsey, the author of the *Total Money Makeover* and David Bach, the author of the *Automatic Millionaire,* who believe the process of using credit cards causes significantly more spending than if you actually handle the cash being spent. Use cash for your incidentals each month. Both Ramsey and Bach believe the charges on the credit slip are psychologically divorced from the reality of spending. It's similar to the act of gambling in Vegas where the actual money is purposely divorced from the chips to encourage more gambling. Bach suggests that before making any large credit card purchase you wait for a 48-hour "cooling off period" to avoid making expensive impulse purchase mistakes.

## Have Debt Troubles?

If you are carrying very large credit card debt and other debts that require service, you may want to consider personal bankruptcy if your situation is dire. It is better to go into retirement with some of your assets intact, than be drained to nothing in a futile, well-intentioned effort to pay everyone. Generally, your employer-sponsored 401(k) and pensions are protected from bankruptcy proceedings, while IRAs just gained protected status in 2005, but the rules are evolving. It is very important to know that your Social Security benefits, if properly handled, are not subject to confiscation by creditors. Your benefits and any benefits received for a dependent child must be deposited into a separate account labeled "Social Security benefits" and not intermingled with any of your other earnings and assets in order to be protected. The only organizations that can take your Social Security check are the IRS (for back taxes) and courts seeking child support payments.

In most states bankruptcy proceedings allow you to retain your home. However, liens against your property for first and second mortgages cannot be wiped away. It is important to avoid consolidating your loans with a line of credit or other lien on your house, if you are considering bankruptcy. The shame of bankruptcy and the destruction of your credit for a few years is not the end of the world. Being destroyed financially, while trying to get out of debt in the later years of your life, without the years to recover from your losses is pretty close to the end of the world.

Chronic and catastrophic illnesses in your family can quickly create huge debt. Bankruptcy can eliminate those debts, but it is not so easy

*continued*

to protect your house if you have a prolonged stay in a nursing home. If you exhaust all your resources and must go on Medicaid, the state health care program for the poor, your house becomes an asset that can be sold to pay your bill. If you are married and have an ailing spouse, transfer the title of your home, and other major assets, into your name in order to keep them.

State laws vary. In some states a spouse can keep the house, but spouses must split other assets. In other states both are in jeopardy. Depending on the state, you may have to plan three years ahead and make the asset transfers, because last minute transfers will not be recognized and assets can be seized. I know this from personal experience. A dear family friend advised us correctly, after my father had a stroke and long before he entered a nursing home, and we transferred titles to family assets.

If things are not that bad and you think that you can work out your debt, beware of the debt management companies that you may see advertised. Many are fraudulent, or at least extremely expensive. Even if they call themselves non-profit, often they are not. Some of these companies charge high hidden fees such as a "voluntary" contribution of your first month's debt payment as a fee to your debt management company. Use the legitimate Consumer Credit Counseling Service at 800-388-2227 to find a reputable agency if you think you need one.

## NANCY'S RETIREMENT EXPENSE INVESTIGATION

Nancy said her advisor suggested that she will need approximately 70 percent of her pre-retirement income during retirement because her expenses would be lower. Nancy considers herself a conservative spender, but the exercise to estimate her expenses was an eye-opener. As a result of our changing perception of retirement and increased healthy life span, retirement has become more expensive than ever. Many common leisure activities are expensive, especially when added to the increased health care costs associated with a longer, more active lifetime.

## NANCY'S ESTIMATE OF RETIREMENT NEEDS

| Monthly Expenses | Basic | Discretionary | Total |
|---|---|---|---|
| *HOUSING:* | | | |
| Rent or mortgage* | $0 | | |
| Insurance (total/12) | $80 | | |
| Maintenance, repairs | $100 | | |
| Utilities | $220 | | |
| Property/school taxes (total/12) | $166 | | |
| | | | |
| *GROCERIES* | $400 | | |
| | | | |
| *TRANSPORTATION:* | | | |
| Car payment | $0 | | |
| Insurance (total/12) | $75 | | |
| Fuel | $80 | | |
| Maintenance, repairs | $175 | | |
| Registration/taxes (total/12) | $5 | | |
| *HEALTH COSTS:* | | | |
| Health insurance premiums | $475 | | |
| Medicare/Medigap | $0 | | |
| Drugs not covered | $32 | | |
| Co-pays | $12 | | |
| Toiletries/cosmetics | $50 | | |
| *PERSONAL INSURANCE PREMIUMS:* | | | |
| Life insurance (total/12) | | $50 | |
| Long term care | | $110 | |
| *ENTERTAINMENT* | | | |
| Dining out | $100 | $250 | |
| Cable TV or satellite TV or radio | | $48 | |
| Vacations (total/12) | | $416 | |

*continued*

| Monthly Expenses | Basic | Discretionary | Total |
|---|---|---|---|
| Internet access | | $29 | |
| Movies and concerts | | $80 | |
| Sporting fees/health club | $45 | | |
| Books/magazines/paper | | $22 | |
| Hobbies | | $60 | |
| Other entertainment | | $20 | |
| CLOTHING | $40 | $60 | |
| INCOME TAXES (TOTAL/12) | | | |
| CHARITABLE DONATIONS | | $40 | |
| GIFTS AND PRESENTS | $40 | $60 | |
| CREDIT CARD DEBT PAYMENTS | $0 | | |
| BANK CHARGES | $5 | | |
| LEGAL AND ACCOUNTING | $21 | | |
| OFFICE SUPPLIES | $5 | | |
| OTHER | $20 | $20 | |
| **Total Monthly Expenses** | **$2,146** | **$1,265** | **$3,411** |
| **Total Yearly Expenses** | **$25,752** | **$15,180** | **$40,932** |

*\* Nancy intends to pay off her small mortgage early.*

Nancy's projection of her retirement expenses doesn't look substantially lower than while working at all. They have by and large remained the same. Nearly four in ten current retirees say their expenses during retirement are equal to their pre-retirement expenses. You need to do your own analysis as Nancy did. The rule of thumb held by many financial planners that you will spend at 70 percent of your pre-retirement rate is not realistic, even though planners have repeated it many times.

Many financial planners believe that in the first five years, your expenses will be 90 percent of pre-retirement expenses, which coincidentally is Nancy's case. In the initial retirement phase, you try to do all those things that you always wanted to do but didn't have the time to get accomplished. In the second phase of retirement you slow down physically and have gotten those initial urges out of the way; in the second phase you spend at a rate of 50 percent of your pre-retirement levels. This is probably the longest period of retirement. In the third phase your health is declining and your health-related expenses go up dramatically. Spending goes back up to 90 percent of pre-retirement levels and more, if you need additional medical care. Again, everyone is different and has different interests and needs; you need to do your own forecast of your retirement needs.

Some suggest that you should have a little part-time job, either paid or volunteer. Not only will it bring a little extra cash. But even if you are simply volunteering for a few hours each week, it will keep you busy—and keep you away from the shopping mall.

This chapter may have been short, but do not skip ahead without estimating your retirement expenses. It serves as a goal for your resources to meet. Without a goal, the next chapter about estimating your income will have no context with which to take action.

### Is a Decision Possible?
No. You know your benefits, breakeven, longevity, the effects of your decision on spousal and dependents' benefits, the effects on your benefits of working during early retirement, income taxes on your benefits, and a detailed estimate of your retirement needs. You could decide, but wait until the next chapter to answer your $100,000 question for sure.

# CHAPTER SIX

# What Are Your Resources to Pay for Retirement? Answering Your $100,000 Question

If you are reading this book you are probably nearing retirement yourself or are reading this for someone who is. I am assuming that you do not have decades to save for your retirement. The five years leading up to retirement are not the time to try to dramatically make up for lost time if you did not save and invest over the years. Rather, it is a time to take stock and make the best of the resources you have, then match your expected income to your expected expenses. As mentioned earlier, the real risk of retirement is outliving your savings and other means of support, both public and private.

Nancy has a pretty sizable and conservative portfolio, approximately 50 percent in stock funds, 40 percent in bond funds, and 10 percent cash. Over the years her financial planner has steered her into some good, conservative mutual funds for both stocks and bonds. She has avoided buying individual stocks based on tips from her friends, articles in the paper, or Internet spam. She has invested any extra cash, not already invested from her paycheck directly into her 401(k), into a money market fund earning 1.25 percent. She keeps this as a rainy-day fund. At the end of the year she draws from this fund to add to her other portfolio holdings. Nancy prudently takes full advantage of her 401(k) at work for its immediate tax savings and for tax-deferred growth of her investments. Because they lack either the education or the money to invest, 43 percent of full-time workers do not participate at all in their employer's 401(k) plans. Only 6 percent contribute the maximum. Less than half of all workers approaching retirement have more that $10,000 in tax-favored retirement investment accounts. The average 401(k) balance is $88,000—heavily skewed by the few who take full advantage of the 401(k) opportunity.

Overall, 26 percent of workers over age 55 report having $100,000 or more in total savings, excluding the equity in their homes, while 34 percent report having less than $50,000 in their nest eggs according to the Employee Benefit Research Institute.

Nancy does not have a company-provided pension plan and did not have one with her previous employers. However, many other retirees are leaving millions in pension plans with previous employers because they have forgotten about them or never claim them for whatever reason. "When you leave a job with a traditional pension, just don't assume you've lost the chance to collect it." (Kelly Greene, WSJ, "Don't Scramble Your Nest Egg," 9/30/02)

Like the majority of investors, the stock market meltdown of 2001 and 2002 wiped away most of Nancy's large gains in the bull market run-up from 1998 to 2000. But she had enough bonds with gains in her portfolio to partially offset her losses. Understandably, she believes her future gains in the stock market or bond market are not so certain. The value of her bond portfolio and equity in her home could decrease if interest rates climb. The Federal Reserve began raising interest rates again in 2004.

Nancy has two portfolios. One is her taxable portfolio, which she has grown through years of hard work plus a small inheritance from her father. Each year the interest, dividends, and capital gains have been taxable on her income tax form.

The other is the tax-deferred portfolio, including her IRAs and her employers' 401(k) and profit-sharing plans. These earnings were not taxed and the interest, dividends, and capital gains have been reinvested. When Nancy withdraws the money during retirement, all the distributions will be taxable unless they come from a Roth IRA. A Roth IRA does not provide a tax benefit for contributing, but the earnings and distributions are tax-free when withdrawn. Hopefully, her tax rate will be lower than the rate she paid while working. The portfolio of investments listed here is net of the amount she intends to use to pay off her remaining mortgage of $35,000.

### NANCY'S TAXABLE PORTFOLIO

| Assets | Value | Yield | Income |
|---|---|---|---|
| Cash | $5,000 | 1.25% | $63 |
| CDs Capital One | $49,000 | 3.25% | $1,593 |
| Cash and short-term fixed investments | $54,000 | | |
| Vanguard Total Bond Market Index Fund | $142,000 | 4.39% | $6,235 |
| Vanguard STAR Fund (60% stocks, 40% bonds) | $25,000 | 2.38% | $595 |
| Dodge & Cox Stock Fund | $7,000 | 1.23% | $86 |
| T. Rowe Price Mid-Cap Value Fund | $2,000 | 0.58% | $12 |
| Fidelity Dividend Growth Fund | $2,000 | 0.79% | $16 |
| Total | $232,000 | | $8,600 |

### NANCY'S TAX DEFERRED PORTFOLIO IN IRAs AND 401(k) VEHICLES

| Stock Funds | Value | Yield | Income |
|---|---|---|---|
| Dodge & Cox Stock Fund | $50,000 | 1.23% | $615 |
| Vanguard 500 Index Fund | $35,000 | 1.55% | $542 |

| Stock Funds | Value | Yield | Income |
|---|---|---|---|
| Pennsylvania Mutual Fund | $30,000 | 0% | |
| Weitz Value Fund | $20,000 | 0.51% | $102 |
| T. Rowe Price Mid-Cap Value | $15,000 | 0.58% | $87 |
| T. Rowe Price Mid-Cap Growth | $15,000 | 0% | |
| Fidelity Dividend Growth | $10,000 | 0.79% | $79 |
| American Funds Cap World Growth & Inc. | $8,000 | 2.34% | $187 |
| Oakmark International Fund | $8,000 | 0.58% | $46 |
| Total Stocks Funds | $191,000 | | |
| **Bond Funds** | | | |
| Vanguard Total Bond Market Index Fund | $37,000 | 4.39% | $1,624 |
| Total IRAs and 401(k) | $228,000 | | $3,282 |

### TOTAL INVESTMENT PORTFOLIO SUMMARY

| | | |
|---|---|---|
| Cash & CD Investments | $54,000 | 12% |
| Bonds Funds | $189,000 | 41% |
| Stocks Funds | $217,000 | 47% |
| **Total** | **$460,000** | 100% |

## PORTFOLIO TRACKING

Although Nancy meets with Kay, her financial planner, once a year for an annual financial checkup, she does not have some-one manage her money. When Nancy first met with her planner, she was amazed at the information that Kay provided her about her portfolio. Kay was a genius! She presented Nancy with impressive graphs about her portfolio's composition and special analysts' information on the funds that she owned. One fund's portfolio manager left the fund unexpectedly the year before, and its performance had lagged since then, yet Nancy never knew about it, and assumed it was due to market conditions and held on to it. A listing also showed that Nancy owned quite a few shares of companies that she didn't realize she owned, and several of her mutual funds owned the same company. After the meeting she was excited about the information and studied the report carefully and noticed it came from Morningstar. The amazing report had come from a website called Morningstar.com.

Nancy visited the website and entered the same information that she had given her planner and, voilà, the same report was produced. She began subscribing to the Morningstar premium service for $12.95 a month and had her portfolio monitored for any updated analysts' reports and any other corporate press releases that might affect her holdings. (Morningstar was rated the #1 portfolio tracker by *Barrons* magazine in 2004.) Her mistake of holding onto the mutual fund that had lost its star portfolio manager cost her $3,800 dollars—enough to pay for monitoring her most important assets for 25 years! If Nancy had decided to pay Kay's fee of 1% of the assets in her taxable accounts, that would have added up to over $2,800 a year, and over a few years that would have added up to some real money. A financial manager does add value for many people who feel very uncomfortable with financial matters, lack any expertise with investing, or are just too busy to manage their own money. But for Nancy, who is comfortable and knowledgeable, Kay's help is not worth a sizable percentage of Nancy's portfolio year in and year out. When they meet annually, they review the performance of the past year and decide if there needs to be a change of allocation among the funds or if a new fund needs to be purchased. Kay is a good sounding board and helps Nancy make good decisions. Nancy pays a $300 fee for this service—money well spent.

Management fees are critically important to your portfolio's longevity. A percentage point or two off your annual return has a huge impact on your ability to pay for your retirement expenses and not run out of money. Portfolio expenses should not exceed 1.2%, according to many experts.

Nancy, a relatively sophisticated investor, feels very comfortable with financial matters, so she takes more control of the decision making for her assets. Many people have a financial planner, which is a perfectly logical and necessary expense for those who do not feel competent in this area. Financial planners can either put your portfolio in order and review it periodically for a fee, or at your option, manage your money for an ongoing management fee. Management fees are negotiable and based on the degree of active management desired.

If you don't know a financial planner, you can find one through a trade association such as the National Association of Personal Financial Advisors (*www.napfa.org*), the Financial Planning Association (*www.fpanet.org*), or the International Association of Registered Financial Consultants (*www.iarfc .org*). Your planner should have at a minimum a CFP designation, the license for certified financial planners. These people have at least three years of experience, pass a two-day exam, and must meet continuing education requirements. Other credentials may include a PFS (personal financial specialist) showing accounting and tax expertise; CFA (chartered financial analyst) investment and portfolio management training; and ChFC (chartered financial consultant) and CLU (chartered life underwriter), both insurance expert designations.

Assuming you have checked out your advisor by getting and following through with references, there are several questions that the *Wall Street Journal* said in October 2004 you must ask your advisor:

1. How is the advisor compensated?
2. If a mutual fund suggested has multiple classes of shares, does my advisor have an incentive to propose one class of shares over another?

3. If the fund has multiple classes of shares, which is the best for me? Some share classes have lower commissions for larger investments. Others have higher up-front charges but lower fees afterwards. The length of your investment time will determine the best approach.
4. Does my advisor have an incentive to recommend one fund or fund group over another?
5. Does my advisor's firm have an incentive to recommend one fund over another? Is the firm itself creating incentives for its advisors such as promotions, perks, or trips to recommend one fund over another?
6. Are the fund's total charges and fees in line with other funds in its category? Index funds have low costs and fees, while actively managed funds in the international and small capitalization areas generally charge more.

Using the Morningstar service and her financial planner, Nancy created a good portfolio by several measures: fund ratings, portfolio expenses, and diversification.

## MORNINGSTAR FUND RATINGS

All the funds in Nancy's portfolio had a 4- or 5-star rating. The stars are awarded to funds by Morningstar based on risk and cost-adjusted performance and investment style. Her funds performed well relative to their peers over short and long periods of time.

### Fund Expenses

Nancy has a good collection of low-cost funds. Her portfolio has a low average expense ratio of 0.45% versus an average expense ratio of 1.17% for similar funds, and lower than the

1.2% upper expense limit mentioned before. The mutual fund expenses charged to her funds are about $1,822 a year as estimated by Morningstar. She asked her advisor the questions previously mentioned and they do not apply, since Nancy makes all her investments directly. Morningstar's X-ray Interpreter described the expenses of her portfolio as follows:

> *The mutual funds in your portfolio tend to have very low expense ratios. This is good, because expense ratios have been shown to be a major factor in mutual-fund performance over the long term.*

Standard & Poor's research shows that low fund expenses correlate well with higher returns. "Few, if any, fund characteristics can be linked to performance more so than the level of expenses," said Phil Edwards, managing director of S&P. "It is important for both investors and financial advisors to keep fund expenses in the forefront of their analysis when assembling a portfolio."

In their study of 17,000 stock-fund share classes, S&P found costs were a critical determinant of fund performance. In their study of one-, three-, five , and ten-year periods ending May 31, 2004, U.S. stock funds with lower-than-average expense ratios performed better than funds with higher-than-average expense ratios in all but one smaller category, the mid-capitalization blend category.

## Portfolio Holdings

At a quick glance you can calculate the percentage of holdings in the major classes in Nancy's portfolio. However, the funds themselves have cash in their portfolios so the actual holdings of Nancy's portfolio in cash is quite a bit higher than the 12 percent she had calculated:

| Cash | 16.88% |
| U.S. Stocks | 36.72% |
| Foreign Stocks | 6.03% |
| Bonds | 40.14% |
| Other | 0.23% |

The funds she owns are in a variety of fund classifications based on the investment style of the portfolio manager and the size of the companies that the funds own. Some managers value sales and earnings growth highly, while others value dividends, cash flow, and asset values. At different stages of bull and bear markets, one style tends to out-perform the other. During the Internet craze in the late 1990s, it was all about growth, and during the bust, value was the darling.

The balance in Nancy's portfolio leans toward the somewhat conservative end of the investment spectrum. She holds a large, diversified fund composed of a balance of short-, intermediate-, and long-term maturing bonds. By staying diversified, the value of her bond fund will not dramatically fluctuate as interest rates fluctuate.

Nancy did not work for a large company that provided her the opportunity to invest in the company stock at a discount in her 401(k). However, having a concentration of your company's stock has its risks, as we have seen in number of dramatic headline-grabbing cases between 2000 and 2005. At Enron where employees were highly concentrated in company stock, they lost not only their 401(k) stock investments, but their jobs as well. Other companies' plans are heavily invested in their own stock. In 2004, 38 percent of the $3.6 billion in assets of the retailer JCPenney's 401(k) program were invested in JCPenney stock. That is risky. JCPenney is a fine company and yours might be too, but you should be aware that you are taking a big risk with your retirement by owning a great deal of your company's stock.

Morningstar's X-ray Interpreter takes all the information it has on your holdings and risks and makes a general description. Morningstar agrees with Nancy's description of her portfolio—it is conservative, but not overly so:

> *Your portfolio is moderately risky. Financial planners typically recommend this type of portfolio for investors who have three- to 10-year investment horizons and who are concerned by volatility but not preoccupied by it. Such portfolios often generate a healthy stream of income.*

In addition to Morningstar.com, in October 2004 Fidelity Investments launched its own online account called Fidelity Income Management Account, with many of the features of Morningstar. Merrill Lynch is planning its own site as well.

## Companies and Market Capitalization

The companies whose stock you own are classified by the size of the company's market capitalization. Capitalization is the total value of the company's equity, taking its share price and multiplying it by the number of shares outstanding. For example, Home Depot in 2004 was trading at $37 per share and had 2.2 billion shares outstanding, which would set its market cap at about $81 billion.

Generally, larger cap companies are more stable because they are more mature and established. Many pay dividends from consistent and predictable cash flows and many analysts follow their day-to-day events and financial reports. However, many new companies may become highly valued as large cap because of investors' anticipation of their futures. Mid caps are generally smaller, more risky, and less mature. Small capitalizations generally have fewer shareholders, even smaller sales, and few, if any, analysts watching them closely. Within each of the three classifications there are many very stable, profitable businesses, but also some very speculative ones. There are funds to match the risk tolerances of their investors.

Morningstar (as well as some fund managers) use a variable, floating system to define market-cap classification cutoffs. Thus, Morningstar defines large-cap to include the largest 70 percent of the market's value. Mid-cap is the next largest 20 percent. And small-cap is the smallest 10 percent of the equity market. As a result, Morningstar's definition of large-, mid-, and small-cap changes slightly from month to month. In March 2004, Morningstar set its cutoff between mid- and large-cap at $8.5 billion, and set the line between mid- and small-cap at $1.5 billion. These thresholds change over time. For example, in March 2000, at the height of the bull market, the line between mid- and large-cap was $11 billion, while at the trough in March 2003 the dividing line was $7.6 billion—a big difference.

Morningstar's X-Ray Interpreter also evaluates the diversity of a portfolio's holdings. Nancy's holdings were given high marks and described as follows:

*Your portfolio's stock exposure is spread evenly across the market and includes a good mix of small, medium, and large companies as well as a fairly even mix of conservatively priced value stocks and high-flying growth stocks. For most investors, maintaining such a broad-based market exposure is a prudent way to invest.*

## NANCY'S PORTFOLIO SHOWN BY INVESTMENT STYLE AND COMPANY SIZE

**Fund Investment Valuation Style**

| Company Size | Value | Blend | Growth |
|---|---|---|---|
| Large | 26% | 18% | 14% |
| Mid-Cap | 9% | 10% | 10% |
| Small | 4% | 6% | 3% |

## NANCY'S PORTFOLIO DETAIL BY FUND CLASSIFICATION

| | | |
|---|---|---|
| Vanguard Total Bond Market Index Fund | $179,000 | Intermediate Bond |
| Dodge & Cox Stock Fund | $57,000 | Large-Cap Value |
| Vanguard 500 Index Fund | $35,000 | Large-Cap Blend |
| Pennsylvania Mutual Fund | $30,000 | Small-Cap Blend |
| Vanguard STAR Balanced Fund | $25,000 | Moderate Allocation |
| Weitz Value Fund | $20,000 | Mid-Cap Value |
| T. Rowe Price Mid-Cap Value Fund | $17,000 | Mid-Cap Value |
| T. Rowe Price Mid-Cap Growth | $15,000 | Mid-Cap Growth |
| Fidelity Dividend Growth Fund | $12,000 | Large-Cap Blend |
| American Funds Cap World Growth & Inc. | $8,000 | World Stock Fund |
| Oakmark International Fund | $8,000 | Foreign Large Cap Value |

An S&P study of ten-year performance found that large-cap growth funds with above-average expenses returned 7.19%, while the below-average expense funds returned 8.9%. The whole spectrum of funds looked as follows:

| LOWER EXPENSE FUNDS PRODUCE HIGHER RETURNS | | |
|---|---|---|
| **S&P Study for the 10-year period ending May 31, 2004** | | |
| | **Above Avg. Expenses** | **Below Avg. Expenses** |
| **Large Cap Growth** | 7.19% | 8.90% |
| Large Cap Blend | 7.93 | 10.01 |
| Large Cap Value | 9.19 | 10.53 |
| Mid Cap Growth | 6.56% | 9.47% |
| Mid Cap Blend | 12.13 | 12.12 |
| Mid Cap Value | 11.01 | 12.21 |
| Small Cap Growth | 6.47% | 10.29% |
| Small Cap Blend | 10.72 | 11.51 |
| Small Cap Value | 11.36 | 13.40 |

*Includes reinvested distributions.*

*Source: In The Vanguard, Autumn, 2004, p. 6.*

## Stocks Held in Common by Your Mutual Funds

A number of pharmaceutical companies including Merck are located around the Philadelphia area, where Nancy lives. A few of Nancy's friends own the company stock through their employer and have done well over the years. Nancy consciously has avoided picking stocks for her portfolio, because she didn't feel that she knew more than the experts did. With any single stock there is the specific risk of owning the company. By owning mutual funds you have the "systematic risk" of owning diversified baskets of stocks that are subject to the systematic ups and the downs of the general stock market. Nancy felt very good about her diversification strategy when Merck announced its recall of Vioxx in October 2004 and shed a third of its value.

However, Nancy owned another big pharmaceutical company and did not even know it. It was Pfizer. Pfizer is a large drug stock, one of thirty stocks in the Dow Jones Industrial Average. Morningstar's analysis called Stock Intersections said that Pfizer was held by four of her funds and makes up 0.39 percent (four-tenths of 1 percent) of her entire portfolio and 4.36 percent of the Fidelity Dividend Growth fund she owned. (If it had been a higher percentage of her entire portfolio, Morningstar would have suggested an adjustment.) Concentrated ownership by her funds in a single stock is followed in decreasing order by Hewlett-Packard, Microsoft, General Electric, AT&T Wireless, Comcast-A, and Time Warner. For example, Pfizer's stock is found in the following funds:

| NANCY'S PORTFOLIO HOLDINGS OF PFIZER | | | |
|---|---|---|---|
| % of Fund | Common Holding/ Funds Holding | Portfolio % | Market Value |
| | Pfizer | 0.39% | $1,806.90 |
| 2.45% | Vanguard 500 Index | 0.19% | $857.50 |
| 4.36% | Fidelity Dividend Growth Fund | 0.11% | $523.20 |
| 0.70% | Dodge & Cox Stock | 0.09% | $399.00 |
| 0.34% | American Funds Capital World G/I | 0.01% | $27.20 |

## TAXES AND THE "INCOME TRAP"

An important issue of portfolio allocation relates to diversification and taxes. If you are too conservative, you may fall into an "income trap" that costs you excess tax expense. Since you must pay taxes on both dividend income and bond interest currently in your taxable portfolio, a balance of income-producing investments and appreciating stocks is the best way to avoid a large tax bite in your taxable portfolio. By owning stocks that can appreciate tax-free until you periodically sell them for current needs, the portfolio minimizes its current tax obligations. Only the portion of the stock sales related to capital gains is taxable. On the other hand, if you relied only on current portfolio income of interest and dividends for your needs, then your entire income each year would be subject to taxes. In your tax-deferred portfolio, a balance of investments is also preferred for diversification purposes rather than tax purposes.

In Nancy's case, she is relying heavily on her income from interest and dividends to provide her the bulk of her current needs outside Social Security. To avoid the income trap that she currently is falling into, she and her planner should plan for a balanced and periodic reduction of her stock portfolio in order to supply a portion of her current needs, minimize taxes, and preserve her portfolio for her lifetime.

## REAL ESTATE INVESTMENTS

Real estate is often the only investment that lower-income seniors have. It acts as a forced savings account when life's excuses have gotten in the way of disciplined savings and investing. Nancy owns her own home and has a small mortgage balance. Real estate prices in the Philadelphia area have been crazy for the past five years and her house has appreciated by 60 percent in that time. As surveyed by Freddie Mac, the large mortgage lending organization, real estate has skyrocketed over 44 percent nationally in the five-year period form 1999 to 2004. If you live in one of the markets that has experienced extraordinary growth, you might want to consider selling and downsizing or moving to a more affordable area.

| PROPERTY VALUES HAVE SOARED IN THE 5 YEARS ENDING 2004 | |
|---|---|
| | Increase |
| Washington, D.C. | 97.4% |
| California | 94.2% |
| Rhode Island | 91.9% |
| Massachusetts | 75.7% |
| New Hampshire | 71.5% |
| New York | 70.8% |
| New Jersey | 70.6% |
| Total U.S. | 44.8% |

Source: Federal Home Mortgage Corp., WSJ, 11/10/04, p. D1.

Nancy purchased a duplex for an investment, and its value has gone up smartly as well, but not to the same degree as her home. (In the Northeast United States a duplex is called a twin home.) She bought it at the beginning of the big run-up on the advice of her cousin, a real estate broker, who spotted the place during a house hunt for a client. The rent covers the expenses and provides a small but nice tax deduction at the end of the year because of the interest and depreciation deductions. She also re-financed the duplex at a very low interest rate in 2003, which helps her keep expenses low.

| HOME EQUITY | |
|---|---|
| 3-Bedroom Home in Montgomery County, Pennsylvania | $220,000 |
| Mortgage on Home | $35,000 |
| Net Equity in Home | $185,000 |

continued

| Investment Property | |
|---|---|
| 2-Bedroom Duplex in Chester County, Pennsylvania | $89,000 |
| Mortgage on Duplex | $59,000 |
| Net Equity in Duplex | $30,000 |

## PORTFOLIO OVERVIEW

Nancy has created quite a large nest egg for herself and is way ahead of the average American. Her portfolio summary is as follows. Currently it generates $8,600 annually from her taxable portfolio and $3,282 from her tax-deferred savings plans.

| NANCY'S PORTFOLIO SUMMARY | |
|---|---|
| Cash & CD Investments | $54,000 |
| Bonds Funds | $189,000 |
| Stocks Funds | $217,000 |
| Real Estate Equity | $215,000 |
| Total | $675,000 |

## CALCULATING NANCY'S OPERATING DEFICIT

In chapter 5, we documented that Nancy's projected expenses are roughly $3,411 a month or $40,932 a year. To match Nancy's expected outflow with her projected income during early retirement, we have to include calculations for the tax liability, since it will reduce her spendable earnings. Calculating taxes prevents a simple calculation, but figuring the taxes is a necessary evil that can't be avoided. The following is a rough illustrative calculation, but it highlights the basic rule that you must consider in your own calculation. It contains a lot of numbers, but the math is very simple. Do not be scared away from it, and try to follow the calculations because they are the most critical in your evaluation to take early Social Security benefits.

## NANCY'S SEMI-RETIREMENT INCOME CALCULATIONS

**Total Income**

| | |
|---|---|
| Wages | $25,000 |
| Interest and dividends | $8,600 |
| Rental profits | $2,300 |
| Total Income | $35,900 |

**Computation of Federal Taxes**

| | |
|---|---|
| Total regular income | $35,900 |
| Less standard deduction | ($4,750) |
| Less exemption | ($3,050) |
| Net taxable income | $28,100 |
| Federal tax at 15% | $4,215 |

**Social Security Taxes on Wages**

| | |
|---|---|
| Wage income | $25,000 |
| Social Security taxes | 6.2% |
| Medicare taxes | 1.45% |
| Total taxes ($25,000 x 7.65%) | $1,912 |

**State Income Taxes***

| | |
|---|---|
| Total regular income | $35,900 |
| State tax at 3% | $1,077 |

**Local Earned Income Tax**

| | |
|---|---|
| Wage income | $25,000 |
| Local tax at 1% | $250 |

*continued*

**Nancy's Semi-Retirement Income Calculation Summary**

| | |
|---|---|
| Total projected income | $35,900 |
| Less total income taxes | $7,454 |
| Net Spendable Income | $28,446 |

*Fifteen states tax Social Security benefits in some way. The list includes CO, CT, IA, KS, MN, MO, MT, NE, NM, ND, RI, UT, VT, WV, and WI.*

So let's take that projected income of $28,446 and subtract her projected expenses of $40,932, leaving an annual operating deficit of $12,486 during her semi-retirement years. The deficit can be closed by Nancy's Social Security benefits and her monthly withdrawals from her nest egg. However, the long-term impact of her decision to collect Social Security on both her early retirement income and her full retirement income needs to calculated.

Should a significant gap remain between income and expense that cannot be filled, Nancy would need to revisit her expense budget as prepared in chapter 5, and evaluate whether her portfolio's income stream from her chapter 6 portfolio could be increased. She would need to cut her expenses or to increase her income by assuming more risk in her portfolio, either by choosing other investments to expand current income or to increase projected appreciation for periodic asset sales.

## DECIDING TO ACCEPT EARLY SOCIAL SECURITY BENEFITS

The calculation of Nancy's annual operating deficit of $12,486 does not include accepting an early retirement check from Social Security. If she worked earning $25,000 as she planned, and collected her annual Social Security benefit, the benefit would be $4,422 a year as calculated before. That reduces her yearly deficit to $8,064 ($12,486 minus $4,422). But let's not take it just yet. Read carefully.

Assuming she rejects her possible annual early Social Security benefit of $4,422 at age 62, and waits until she reaches her full retirement age at 66, her income with a full Social Security benefit and no part-time employment would look like this:

| FULL RETIREMENT INCOME CALCULATIONS AT AGE 66 | |
| --- | --- |
| *Full* Social Security | $16,260 |
| (no deductions, full benefits) | |
| Interest and dividends | $8,600 |
| Rental profits | $2,300 |
| | $27,160 |
| | |
| **Computation of Federal Taxes\*** | |
| Total regular income | $10,900 |
| Less standard deduction | ($4,750) |
| Less exemption | ($3,050) |
| Net taxable income | $3,100 |
| Federal tax at 10% | $310 |
| | |
| **State Income Taxes** | |
| Total regular income | $10,900 |
| State tax at 3% | $327 |
| | |
| **Local Earned Income Tax** | |
| Wage income | $0 |
| Local tax at 1% | $0 |
| | |
| **Retirement Projection** | |
| Total projected income | $27,160 |
| Less total income taxes | $627 |
| Net spendable income | $26,523 |

*continued*

**Semi-Retirement Projection**

| | |
|---|---|
| Total projected income | $35,900 |
| Less total income taxes | $7,454 |
| Net spendable income | $28,446 |

*There are no taxes on her Social Security benefits as the calculated Base Amount is $19,030, which is less than the Annual Earnings Test's $25,000 limit. Compare that to her semi-retirement years without Social Security benefits and there is not that much of a difference.*

Stay with me here, this is where it all comes together. You are almost at the end of the O. Henry short story with a surprise ending. You are about to look beyond her four years of early retirement, and see the price she will pay for the rest of her retirement years for her decision to take early retirement—if she decides to. The price is astronomically high unless Nancy believes that she will have a very short life.

Remember Nancy does have the option of working and taking the early Social Security retirement annual benefits of $4,422 for four years between age 62 and age 66. If she does choose early retirement benefits, her full retirement picture without working at age 66 would look like this:

| FULL RETIREMENT INCOME CALCULATION *WITH REDUCED* SOCIAL SECURITY BENEFITS | |
|---|---|
| Reduced Social Security | $11,568 |
| Interest and dividends | $8,600 |
| Rental profits | $2,300 |
| Total Projected Income | $22,468 |
| Less total income taxes | $637 |
| **Net Spendable Income w/Benefits Reduced** | **$21,831** |

If she does not take early Social Security benefits, then her retirement picture looks like this:

| FULL RETIREMENT INCOME CALCULATION *WITH FULL* SOCIAL SECURITY BENEFITS | |
|---|---|
| Full Social Security | $16,260 |
| Interest and dividends | $8,600 |
| Rental profits | $2,300 |
| Total Projected Income | $27,160 |
| Less total income taxes | $637 |
| **Net Spendable Income w/ *Full* Benefits** | **$26,523** |
| **Annual Difference** | **$4,692** |

What does this long calculation means for Nancy? If she accepts the early Social Security benefits of $4,422 a year from ages 62 to 66, Nancy would be giving up annual benefits of $4,692 a year, plus annual adjustments for inflation for all of her retirement years thereafter. Her break-even time period is very short. If Nancy waits until age 66 to retire, it will take her just four years at the increased benefit level to receive the entire amount she would have collected in early retirement between the ages of 62 to 66. So if Nancy estimates that she will live past age 70 (that's four years in full retirement) she will not only surpass her entire early retirement income, but she will enjoy an extra $4,692 a year for the rest of her life! That is $391 of extra spending money per month (annually indexed upward for inflation) for Nancy to spend on entertainment, prescription drugs, or whatever she decides. Obviously, taking early retirement benefits would be a costly mistake for Nancy.

If Nancy lives to age 83 (using just a 2% inflation rate) *she would be making a $100,000 mistake by taking early Social Security benefits.* Coincidentally, that is exactly what her projected life span is per the Period Life Table mentioned in the introduction of this book. If Nancy lives to a ripe old age of 93, opting for early Social Security benefits would be a huge $200,000 error!

| HOW NANCY WILL BE $100,000 AHEAD BY CHOOSING FULL SOCIAL SECURITY BENEFITS | | | | | |
|---|---|---|---|---|---|
| | **Age 62** | **Age 66** | **Age 70** | **Age 83** | **Age 93** |
| Full Benefits | $0 | $26,523 | $26,523 | $26,523 | $26,523 |
| Reduced Early Benefits | $4,422 | $21,831 | $21,831 | $21,831 | $21,831 |
| Cumulative Difference | ($4,422) | ($17,688) | $0 | +$100,000 | +$200,000 |

## OTHER FACTORS TO CONSIDER

There are other factors you need to consider for your own calculation for retirement that did not pertain to Nancy. If you do not earn significant wages during your early retirement years, you will not be subject to deductions of the Annual Earnings Test. Your early retirement benefits would be reduced only by the standard reductions for retiring early. In that case the break-even ages in the break-even tables in chapter 1 apply to you, as do your evaluations of your longevity in chapter 2. These would lead you to your right answer.

If you plan on receiving a significant early retirement check, you may have the opportunity to invest that check if you have enough other retirement savings. Or you may defer the use of your other investments so they could continue to grow in a 401(k) or IRA. If you do, you would need to add those earnings estimates, net of possible taxes, to your calculation to favor accepting early benefits at age 62. If you have few savings that could be invested and you need your benefits to make ends meet, then you do not add these benefits to your early retirement calculation. But in that case, it would be best to continue working until full retirement. You would maximize your benefits, avoid early retirement deductions, and contribute additional years to Social Security.

It should be pointed out that Nancy's example is a relatively simple one. It provides you with a general framework so you can answer your own $100,000 question. It is not a cookie cutter that can be used in all situations. Well-trained professionals can help you resolve complicated tax issues and show you how to reduce your taxes. A financial planner can look at your expenses and income, and provide projections that may be difficult for you to estimate. These calculations and projections are extremely important to your future, so if you feel overwhelmed by them, don't hesitate to seek professional advice. By reading this book you already know how the financial professionals you may hire will approach your financial planning assignment, and you will be a better, more knowledgeable consumer of their services. If your situation is relatively simple, this book alone will have you speeding on your way to a happy and more prosperous retirement.

What's to be learned from Nancy's example and the $100,000 question process:

1. If you are planning to work during early retirement and will earn substantial income, make sure to calculate your net benefits after all taxes and Social Security penalties.
2. Evaluate your health and make a life-span estimate, knowing full well that you may live longer or shorter than the average lifetime.
3. If you are married or have other dependents who will be collecting based on your work record, evaluate what ef-

fect your early retirement decision will have on their benefits.

4. If you decide to retire early, consider the high cost of medical insurance until you turn 65 when you become eligible for inexpensive Medicare health coverage.

5. Calculate your early retirement cash needs and compare them with your projected income to determine if you can afford four additional years of saving less and spending more from your nest egg.

The last point, regardless of your early retirement decision, is extremely important. Creating an investment withdrawal plan that minimizes your chance to run out of money is the key to your successful retirement and your peace of mind. It may be a simple concept in theory but it has many complexities, as the next chapter will explain.

## The Retire Early? $100,000 Question Worksheets

### Calculation of Your Annual Spendable
### Income and Social Security Alternatives

This worksheet pulls together the information in the book so that you can answer your own $100,0000 question concerning Social Security, and can begin planning for your financial future in retirement. In the first column you estimate your income during your early retirement years. In the second column you will do the same for your full retirement years. These are estimates, so do not get hung up on getting it exactly right, just go through the process.

In this chapter you have the tools to estimate your spendable income. You may decide to work full time, part time, or not at all. Then you will estimate the taxes that will be paid to the federal, state, and local governments. To determine your investment income you must analyze your nest egg with financial tools such as Morningstar as shown.

| Taxable Income Calculation | Early Retirement Age 62 to NRA | | Full Retirement NRA and thereafter | |
|---|---|---|---|---|
| Wages | $ | | $ | |
| Investment income | $ | | $ | |
| Other | $ | | $ | |
| Taxable Income | $ | | $ | |

**Federal Income Tax Calculation**

| | | | | |
|---|---|---|---|---|
| Taxable income | $ | | $ | |
| Less Standard Deduction* | ( | ) | ( | ) |
| Less Personal Exemptions* | ( | ) | ( | ) |
| Adjusted Income | $ | | $ | |
| Multiplied by the Tax Rate* | × | % | × | % |
| Federal Tax | $ | | $ | |

\* Consult a tax guide or www.irs.org for your applicable standard deduction, exemptions, and tax rates. If you have many deductions and itemize, use your total deductions.

**Social Security and Medicare Taxes on Wages**

| | | | | |
|---|---|---|---|---|
| Wages | $ | | $ | |
| Multiplied by the Tax Rate of 7.65%** | × | % | × | % |
| SS and Medicare Taxes | $ | | $ | |

\*\* If self-employed use 15.3% because you pay both the employee and employer portion of the tax.

**State Taxes Calculation**

| | | | | |
|---|---|---|---|---|
| Taxable Income*** | $ | | $ | |
| Less Standard Deduction | ( | ) | ( | ) |
| Less Personal Exemptions | ( | ) | ( | ) |
| Adjusted Income | $ | | $ | |
| Multiplied by the Tax Rate | × | % | × | % |
| State Tax | $ | | $ | |

\*\*\* Fifteen states tax Social Security benefits in some way. The list includes CO, CT, IA, KS, MN, MO, MT, NE, NM, ND, RI, UT, VT, WV, and WI. Consult your state's tax return for standard deductions, exemptions, and tax rate.

Local Tax Calculation

| | | | | |
|---|---|---|---|---|
| Wages | $ | | $ | |
| Multiplied by the Tax Rate**** | × | % | × | % |
| Total Local Taxes | $ | | $ | |

**** Consult your local tax return for tax rate and any other particulars of your locality.

Spendable Income Calculation

| | | | | |
|---|---|---|---|---|
| Total Taxable Income | $ | | $ | |
| Less Total Taxes from above | ( | ) | ( | ) |
| Spendable Income | $ | | $ | |

## Comparison of Social Security Benefit Alternatives

In this section you will gather the information you have found about your Social Security benefits in the previous chapters: your Social Security statement in chapter 1, your dependents benefits in chapter 3, and the penalties and taxes on your benefits for working while collecting benefits in chapter 4. In the second column you will place your estimates of benefits during early retirement. Then you will compare that estimate with your estimates of what your full retirement benefits would be.

| | Early Retirement Age 62 to NRA | | Full Retirement NRA and thereafter | |
|---|---|---|---|---|
| | No Benefits | Reduced Benefits | Full Benefits | Reduced Benefits |
| **Benefits** | | | | |
| Social Security benefits (chapters 1 and 4) | $0 | $ | $ | $ |
| Dependents SS benefits (chapters 3 and 4) | $0 | $ | $ | $ |
| Less income taxes, on SS for "Upper Incomes" (see chapter 4 worksheet) | $0 | $( ) | $( ) | $( ) |
| Total Benefits | $0 | $A | $B | $C |
| | | Age 62 to NRA (4 to 5 years) | NRA and beyond (? years) | |

With this line of "Total Benefits" information, compare the "Early Retirement" benefits and the two "Full Retirement" benefit scenarios. Divide the *total* additional early benefits (A × Years of Early Retirement) by the *annual* increase in benefits for waiting and you have the number of years to break even (B − C). Look to your own analysis of longevity in Chapter 2 to see if it is likely you will live past the "Break-even Years." If you estimate that you will live past the "Break-even Years," wait for full benefits.

$$\frac{(\$A) \times \text{Years of Early Retirement}}{B - C} = \text{Break-even Years}$$

### Planning Your Financial Future

Continuing with your retirement planning process, the following information shows the full impact of your projected income, projected expenses, and choice of Social Security benefits on your annual cash flow during retirement. Use this information to get an idea of what you need from your nest egg to support yourself. If your nest egg cannot support you, then you may need to reconsider the decision to retire early, your spending plans and the allocation of your portfolio.

| | Early Retirement Age 62 to NRA | | Full Retirement NRA and thereafter | |
|---|---|---|---|---|
| | No Benefits | Reduced Benefits | Full Benefits | Reduced Benefits |
| Spendable Income (from above) | $ | $ | $ | $ |
| Total Benefits (from above) | $0 | $ | $ | $ |
| Less Living Expenses (chapter 5) | ( ) | ( ) | ( ) | ( ) |
| Less Medicare Premium (www.medicare.gov) | ( ) | ( ) | ( ) | ( ) |
| Annual Nest Egg Requirements | $ | $ | $ | $ |
| | Age 62 to NRA (4 to 5 years) | | NRA and beyond ( ? years ) | |

# CHAPTER SEVEN

# Tapping Your Retirement Nest Egg: How to Make Ends Meet?

Investing *for* retirement is totally different from investing *during* retirement. On your march to retirement you want to maximize your nest egg by taking on a measure of risk. This is what financial planners advise, and so do I. During retirement, the goal is to generate sufficient income so you won't run out of money. Conversely, if you withdraw too little, you may be needlessly lowering your standard of living. Therefore, the important questions after the big $100,000 question about benefits are:

> *How much can I safely withdraw each year from my portfolio?*
> *Have I saved enough to retire without running out of money?*
> *How should I alter my investment strategy when I retire?*

The traditional withdrawal plan during retirement was a simple calculation. Take what you have as your pre-retirement nest egg, guess what you are going to earn on average, and then try to match the withdrawal rate so that you don't run out of money. A recent Fidelity Investments survey found that on average, respondents expected to withdraw 6% of their savings, with almost one third expecting to withdraw 7% or more annually. In theory, if you project earnings of 8% a year and take 4% a year from the portfolio, you will not dip into the nest egg, so you will leave a nice inheritance. This is the basis of countless retirement calculators used by planners and available for free on Web sites. And guess what? They are wrong. The problem is that the markets do not work that way. The market does not produce "average" returns. Real returns depend on the point of entry and exit and all the ups and downs in between. In statistical terms, that unpredictability is called volatility. That is why even the returns of a conservative portfolio of investments do not plot in a straight line. Even the highly rated Dodge & Cox Stock Fund, a fairly conservative portfolio of stocks with a stellar long-term record, had a 10.5 percent loss in 2002. If you combine the growth potential of stocks with more predictable bonds, the total return may be lower, but the volatility or risk will be diminished.

Bonds are not the only answer. If you remember the inflation of the late 1970s, interest rates spiked up to 18% and the value of bonds was crushed. When interest rates rise, the value of bonds falls. So do not assume that an all-bond portfolio is the answer. The goal is to diversify your portfolio to lower the risk and still get a good, if not always the maximum, return.

## HISTORICAL STUDIES

In 1995 professors Cooley, Hubbard, and Walz of Trinity University in Texas performed an often quoted study known as the Trinity Study. They took historical information from 1926 to 1995 and back tested many portfolios of stocks and bonds to determine what probability there was of exhausting a portfolio if you earned X and withdrew Y each year. During the years studied there were forty-one different 30-year time periods. A 25 percent failure rate, for example, means that the portfolio failed ten of the forty-one periods studied. For periods of 15 and years, 20 years, and 25 years there were fifty-six, fifty-one, and forty-six different periods, respectively, that were studied.

The study's usefulness lies in its demonstration of the relationship between time horizon, asset allocation, and withdrawal rates. Historic studies are somewhat limited and should be used as a guide and not a security blanket. Historical back testing relies on the assumption that past results not only reoccur on average, but also reoccur in exactly the same sequence as in the past. This time-path sequence assumption is very risky, but it is a start and better than nothing.

The Trinity Study took 30-, 25-, 20-, and 15-year time horizons as mentioned and considered failure as running out of money. In one set of data the study took the same percentage of the initial portfolio and adjusted upward for inflation each year. In another set of data the study took the same percentage of the initial portfolio and kept the withdrawal amount the same each year. In the following charts that I created for this book, I combined the data for inflation-adjusted withdrawals and the data of steady withdrawals and presented them together for easy comparison. The charts also show where a portfolio may fail.

Using the 30-year withdrawal data you are implicitly projecting a 92-year life span (62 + 30) if you retire early, or 96 with full retirement. If you refer back to the second chapter you can estimate your own longevity and chose the appropriate chart. Remember that the averages are just averages, and your longevity estimate has a 50 percent chance being too long or too short. Twenty-eight percent of all men at age 65 will live to be 90. Forty percent of all 65-year-old women will live to be 90 years old. That is why the 30-year projection is a reasonable choice to reference in your planning. If you want to be conservative, you should choose the longer 30-year withdrawal period to ensure you do not outlive your resources. If you have information that leads you to think your years are fewer or you are able to deal with a greater probability of failure, use a shorter time period.

If you chose the 25-year withdrawal data, you implicitly project an 87-year life span (62 + 25) if you retire early, or 91 with full retirement. Using the 20-year withdrawal data, you implicitly project an 82-year life span (62 + 20) if you retire early, or 86 with full retirement. Using the 15-year withdrawal data you implicitly project a 77-year life span (62 + 15) if you retire early, or 81 at full retirement.

What you see in the following charts is how the upward adjustment of your annual withdrawal for inflation, will decrease your portfolio to the point of failure. If you feel that your increases in annual expenses do not mirror the Consumer Price Index as a measure of inflation, and may be less, you can assume that you fall between the "adjusted" and the "same $" withdrawal annual amount. In an example pointed out by John Waggoner in *USA Today* in October 8, 2004:

> *The Consumer Price Index increased 2.7% over the past year. Assuming inflation stays at 2.7% and that you withdraw the $1,000 a month, after 10 years the $1,000 will have the current buying power of $896. After 30 years, your $1,000 will be worth $452. To keep up with inflation, you'll have to increase your annual withdrawals.*

Waggoner astutely points out that Social Security benefits are indexed for inflation, making Social Security a very valuable income stream that is hard to duplicate.

## RETIREMENT PORTFOLIO FAILURE RATES OVER 30 YEARS

Adjusted annually for inflation and not adjusted

| Portfolio Composition | Withdrawal Rate of Initial Portfolio | | | | | | | |
| --- | --- | --- | --- | --- | --- | --- | --- | --- |
| | 3% | 4% | 5% | 6% | 7% | 8% | 9% | 10% |
| 100% stocks adjusted | 0% | 5% | 15% | 32% | 41% | 59% | 66% | 66% |
| same $ | 0% | 2% | 5% | 10% | 15% | 22% | 32% | 46% |
| 75% stocks/25% bonds adj. | 0% | 2% | 17% | 32% | 51% | 66% | 78% | 93% |
| same $ | 0% | 0% | 2% | 5% | 12% | 27% | 46% | 54% |
| 50% stocks/50% bonds adj. | 0% | 5% | 24% | 49% | 83% | 95% | 100% | 100% |
| same $ | 0% | 0% | 0% | 2% | 10% | 49% | 63% | 85% |
| 25% stocks/75% bonds adj. | 0% | 29% | 73% | 80% | 95% | 100% | 100% | 100% |
| same $ | 0% | 0% | 0% | 0% | 68% | 95% | 100% | 100% |
| 100% bonds adjusted | 0% | 80% | 83% | 88% | 100% | 100% | 100% | 100% |
| same $ | 0% | 0% | 49% | 73% | 100% | 100% | 100% | 100% |

Source: Trinity Study, American Association of Individual Investors, AAII Journal 2/98

## RETIREMENT PORTFOLIO FAILURE RATES OVER 25 YEARS

Adjusted annually for inflation and not adjusted

| Portfolio Composition | Withdrawal Rate of Initial Portfolio | | | | | | | |
| --- | --- | --- | --- | --- | --- | --- | --- | --- |
| | 3% | 4% | 5% | 6% | 7% | 8% | 9% | 10% |
| 100% stocks adjusted | 0% | 0% | 13% | 30% | 41% | 54% | 65% | 70% |
| same $ | 0% | 2% | 4% | 9% | 13% | 22% | 30% | 50% |
| 75% stocks/25% bonds adj. | 0% | 0% | 15% | 35% | 50% | 63% | 70% | 88% |
| same $ | 0% | 0% | 2% | 4% | 9% | 22% | 43% | 54% |
| 50% stocks/50% bonds adj. | 0% | 0% | 20% | 43% | 63% | 80% | 93% | 100% |
| same $ | 0% | 0% | 0% | 2% | 4% | 30% | 57% | 78% |
| 25% stocks/75% bonds adj. | 0% | 7% | 52% | 76% | 85% | 96% | 98% | 100% |
| same $ | 0% | 0% | 0% | 0% | 22% | 78% | 91% | 100% |
| 100% bonds adjusted | 0% | 54% | 83% | 95% | 89% | 98% | 100% | 100% |
| same $ | 0% | 0% | 2% | 48% | 74% | 93% | 98% | 100% |

Source: Trinity Study, American Association of Individual Investors, AAII Journal 2/98.

## RETIREMENT PORTFOLIO FAILURE RATES OVER 20 YEARS

Adjusted annually for inflation and not adjusted

| Portfolio Composition | Withdrawal Rate of Initial Portfolio | | | | | | | |
|---|---|---|---|---|---|---|---|---|
| | 3% | 4% | 5% | 6% | 7% | 8% | 9% | 10% |
| 100% stocks adjusted | 0% | 0% | 12% | 25% | 37% | 47% | 57% | 67% |
| same $ | 0% | 2% | 4% | 6% | 8% | 16% | 27% | 39% |
| 75% stocks/25% bonds adj. | 0% | 0% | 10% | 25% | 39% | 49% | 63% | 73% |
| same $ | 0% | 0% | 0% | 4% | 6% | 12% | 29% | 49% |
| 50% stocks/50% bonds adj. | 0% | 0% | 10% | 25% | 45% | 67% | 78% | 90% |
| same $ | 0% | 0% | 0% | 0% | 4% | 12% | 39% | 59% |
| 25% stocks/75% bonds adj. | 0% | 0% | 18% | 53% | 69% | 84% | 92% | 96% |
| same $ | 0% | 0% | 0% | 0% | 0% | 29% | 76% | 88% |
| 100% bonds adjusted | 0% | 10% | 53% | 80% | 86% | 88% | 90% | 98% |
| same $ | 0% | 0% | 0% | 4% | 53% | 65% | 84% | 94% |

Source: Trinity Study, American Association of Individual Investors, AAII Journal 2/98.

## RETIREMENT PORTFOLIO FAILURE RATES OVER 15 YEARS

Adjusted annually for inflation and not adjusted

| Portfolio Composition | Withdrawal Rate of Initial Portfolio | | | | | | | |
|---|---|---|---|---|---|---|---|---|
| | 3% | 4% | 5% | 6% | 7% | 8% | 9% | 10% |
| 100% stocks adjusted | 0% | 0% | 0% | 9% | 21% | 30% | 37% | 45% |
| same $ | 0% | 0% | 2% | 2% | 7% | 9% | 12% | 23% |
| 75% stocks/25% bonds adj. | 0% | 0% | 0% | 5% | 18% | 32% | 36% | 54% |
| same $ | 0% | 0% | 0% | 0% | 4% | 5% | 9% | 21% |
| 50% stocks/50% bonds adj. | 0% | 0% | 0% | 7% | 21% | 36% | 50% | 68% |
| same $ | 0% | 0% | 0% | 0% | 0% | 2% | 9% | 29% |
| 25% stocks/75% bonds adj. | 0% | 0% | 0% | 11% | 30% | 50% | 68% | 82% |
| same $ | 0% | 0% | 0% | 0% | 0% | 0% | 9% | 50% |
| 100% bonds adjusted | 0% | 0% | 0% | 29% | 61% | 79% | 82% | 84% |
| same $ | 0% | 0% | 0% | 0% | 0% | 21% | 57% | 62% |

Source: Trinity Study, American Association of Individual Investors, AAII Journal 2/98.

In our example Nancy Kessler has a portfolio of roughly 50 percent stocks and 50 percent bonds. According to the Trinity Study she has a 24% probability that in 30 years her nest egg will be gone if she withdraws 5% each year and adjusts upward for inflation. At a 4% annual withdrawal rate, the failure rate falls to 5%. If she keeps the withdrawal the same, there is next to no probability of failure in either scenario.

The Trinity Study concluded that bonds increased the success rates of portfolios with moderate withdrawal rates, and that most retirees would benefit from 50 percent allocation in stocks to increase returns without much added risk. Retirees who want to adjust their withdrawals for inflation, must accept a lower withdrawal rate from their initial portfolio.

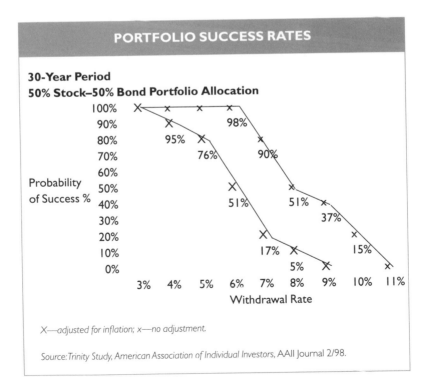

**PORTFOLIO SUCCESS RATES**

**30-Year Period**
**50% Stock–50% Bond Portfolio Allocation**

Probability of Success %

Withdrawal Rate

X—adjusted for inflation; x—no adjustment.

Source: Trinity Study, American Association of Individual Investors, AAII Journal 2/98.

A study conducted by the Web site RetireEarly.com took data from 1871 to 1998 and drew similar conclusions. They concluded that withdrawal rates of 4 to 5% of a retirement portfolio is safe, but rates above 5% increase the probability that a portfolio will be exhausted during a retiree's lifetime. Even if a higher rate were mathematically feasible, a lower rate provides a degree of flexibility just in case the markets take a turn at the most inopportune time. A *Kiplinger's* article, "Make Your Savings Last a Lifetime" in March 2001, advised that "if you want to be sure your money will last at least 30 years, set your initial spending at no more than 4% to 5% of your assets." In a March 10, 2004, *Wall Street Journal* article, Jonathan Clements, quoted financial planners who advised a more conservative 3.5%, 4.1%, and 5% withdrawal rates. In the September 2004 *Employee Benefit News,* Tom Anderson said "most financial planners recommend retirees withdraw 4 percent or less annually from savings to make their retirement investment last." These experts had the benefit of living through the ups and downs of the 1998 to 2003 period.

A study by T. Rowe Price as reported by *Kiplinger's Retirement Report* in March 2001, showed how a simple calculation using averages can go wrong. "Say you retired with a $250,000 portfolio consisting of 60% stocks, 30% bonds and 10% cash. After gauging that the portfolio's annualized returns would average 11.7% over the next 30 years, you decide to tap 8.5% in the first year and adjust annually for inflation.

"The results, the account was drained in 12 years because actual returns were significantly less than the 11.7% average. During 1973–1974 bear market, investors were hard hit with a decline of 17% in 1973 and 28% in 1974." When you keep withdrawing during a downturn you do not regain the losses when the market recovers. "If the original withdrawal rate had been set at a more modest 6%, that same portfolio would have lasted 27 years, just shy of the 30-year goal." Also, in this time period there was a surge of inflation. "If you increased your withdrawals to keep up with inflation, the portfolio would be wounded by the market dive and given a knock-out punch by the increasing large withdrawals for inflation." In the meltdown of 2000 the market got crushed, but fortunately for retirees, portfolios did not get floored by inflation, which was near zero.

"Problems or successes in the early years have dramatic effects. Let's flip this example on its head and assume the returns from 1968 to 1998 were reversed. The first years enjoy the high returns of the 1990s and the rough years come at the end of the period. By the time the last year with 1968's bad data comes, even with a withdrawal rate of 8.5%, the $250,000 grows to $1.2 million. In sum, high returns or high losses at the beginning of the period of retirement have a dramatic effect of the ability on the portfolio's ability to survive."

It's important not to put your plan on autopilot. You must be willing to do midcourse corrections if returns or spending projections change. Monitor your path annually. Just as the consensus of "experts" have changed their advice downward from 5% of 4% or less annually, you too must adjust your plan. The discipline of an initial low withdrawal rate helps new retirees to manage their spending through their first years out of work, avoids crushing their portfolio if those initial years have poor returns, and allows withdrawals based on investment returns and spending needs.

## MONTE CARLO STUDIES

Rather than basing plans on market averages, the Monte Carlo approach uses estimates based on probabilities. Using powerful computer programs, technology has taken the historical studies a step forward. In back testing, the historical results were kept in time sequence, but in Monte Carlo studies, each year's returns are maintained separately in pools. It's a little like a roulette wheel, where each year is a different spoke of the wheel, hence the reference to the historic gambling capital of Europe. The Monte Carlo simulator draws the pools of returns for many sequences randomly based on return and volatility. It does it thousands of times and creates a distribution or graph of the possible results. It is like living the lives of thousands of people all at once and trying to find out how real results, not average results, would occur.

Frank Armstrong of Investor Solutions, Inc., explained it best, "Suppose we expect a portfolio to be worth $100,000 at the end of a period for a particular withdrawal rate, rate of return, and time horizon. If one result yielded $1,000,000, and nine yielded $0 at some particular risk level, we have achieved our average return. But nine out of ten retirees are broke!"

Monte Carlo analysis shows that when the projected volatility increases by the addition of more volatile investments, there may be the same mathematical "average" return, but the median is less than the average. In other words, if you line up all the results side by side, the actual middle (median) results of real individual results are less. In the extreme volatile series of data in the example, $0, $0, $0, $0, $0, $0, $0, $0, $0, $1,000,000, the average is $100,000, but the median result is $0. If you were relying on the $100,000 average to be your result in retirement and you earn $0, you are not only going to be upset at your financial planner, but you are also going to be bankrupt.

If you have a sophisticated financial advisor, he or she may already have a Monte Carlo simulator to wow you with. A simplified version of a Monte Carlo simulator is available at Troweprice.com at the area labeled Retirement Income Calculator (*www.troweprice.com*). This is a key tool that's available to you so you can get an idea about your own portfolio and withdrawal rate. By the way, Morningstar highly rates many of the T. Rowe Price mutual funds. Another sophisticated model available for free is called "The Retirement Probability Analyzer" provided by the Society of Actuaries Web site at *www.soa.org*. The model created by Toronto finance professor, Moshe Milevsky, uses partial differential equations to calculate the "probability of ruin" as he calls the demise of a retirement portfolio.

## WHAT DO THESE VALUABLE STUDIES TEACH US?

1. If your nest egg is not as big as you desire when you begin retirement, you may be tempted to increase your withdrawal rate to meet your expenses. Yet a higher withdrawal rate increases your chances of early disaster.
2. If your nest egg is not as big as you would like, you might reach for higher returns with riskier investments. That increases your volatility which, in turn, increases your chances of reaching zero funds long before your demise.

Therefore, it is more prudent to choose a lower initial withdrawal rate; select a less volatile, more diversified portfolio; and adjust your spending and/or increase your earnings to compensate for a nest egg deficit.

## GOALS FOR YOUR PORTFOLIO

Since everyone's goals are different, there is no single withdrawal rate to suit all needs. Some wish to leave an inheritance for their kids and grandchildren. Others with fewer resources have more at stake if they make any incorrect assumptions in choosing their withdrawal rate. Never overlook or underestimate the need to sleep at night. When you are retired with plenty of time on your hands and no paycheck coming in, anxiety over your financial health can wreck an otherwise pleasant retirement. Whether you are planning for retirement or have entered retirement, you must know your tolerance for risk. If retirement resources are tight compared to your expenses, then a conservative withdrawal rate makes sense.

## Two-Bucket and Three-Bucket Strategies

Frank Armstrong, president of Investors Solutions, encourages an ingenious "two-bucket strategy" to create a less risky portfolio. One bucket is filled with risk-free bonds and the other with stocks. The first bucket is a relatively risk-free portfolio of short-term bonds enough to cover five to seven years of your needs. The second bucket is a well-diversified portfolio of world stocks. By having wide diversification, the volatility of the returns is reduced, but the higher returns of equities are maintained. If the stock market dives, the retiree dips into the first (bond) bucket to pay for current expenses. In this way, beaten-down stocks have the chance to recover. When equity returns are higher, you take profits and make more withdrawals from the second equity portfolio bucket.

Using Armstrong's method, you transition your portfolio in the five to seven years preceding retirement to create the two buckets. Bond holdings become more short-term and equities become more diversified. The years of trying to maximize your nest egg before retirement transitions to the goal of securely generating income. The drawbacks of this method are that you need a sizable portfolio to create a short-term bucket of five to seven years' worth of expenses and a larger bucket of equities. Also, if equities have a prolonged downturn, you would need to lower your withdrawal rate.

In a three-bucket strategy promoted by national financial radio host Ray Lucia, you have three buckets instead of two to better match your investments with your need to provide income, growth, and safety. The first bucket is in short-term investments of CDs and other short-term instruments to provide current income for five years. In the intermediate bucket is another current five years of income invested in stocks and bonds with enough money to grow into seven years' worth of spending in five years. (I calculated that would require a 7% annual return.) Add buckets one and two, and you would have twelve years of spending. The third, long-term bucket would be the rest of your portfolio, invested in stocks with a 12-year time horizon that in theory will double in value by the time buckets one and two are depleted in twelve years. (I calculate that would take a 6% annual return.) That third bucket would then be divided into three buckets, just as you did at the beginning, twelve years earlier. The Lucia theory is to have safe money as well as money that's invested in the market to keep pace with inflation.

## Variable Withdrawal Strategy

Many of the withdrawal strategies have a withdrawal rate from a portfolio that contains various investments. The rate either is a fixed percentage, or is adjusted for inflation. If your portfolio is large enough to cover your needs, or if your needs have a high variable component, you may want to consider a variable withdrawal rate.

To see it another way, instead of taking a fixed percentage of the original portfolio at retirement, which would give you a fixed dollar amount, you would withdraw a fixed percentage of the *remaining* portfolio, which would result in a variable dollar amount. In theory, this method would lead to a very long payout because the withdrawal will get smaller if the portfolio dwindles. It is a way to preserve more principle. It works if you can live on the smaller withdrawals.

Using this method, a high net worth individual would tailor

his or her spending to the withdrawal amount for that year. Instead taking three annual trips, maybe two would be sufficient or charitable donations could be cut back in lean years.

## NANCY'S FULL RETIREMENT PICTURE

Nancy's portfolio has a value of $460,000 and real estate equity of $215,000. The real estate provides Nancy her shelter, so disposing of it would not be the best thing unless she wants to downsize. She can decide what to do with this asset later in life, especially if she has health care needs. Whenever she sells her home, up to $250,000 of the gain is exempt from taxes.

Her duplex investment is working like a tax-free account, because its appreciation is not taxed until sold. The rental income pays her mortgage and the declining balance alone creates equity over time for her. Selling the duplex in Chester County would trigger taxes on the gain, since it is not her primary residence. However, rental property gains can be deferred if the proceeds are reinvested in another property. Nancy can also consider selling this investment in the future.

Nancy is a very conservative and independent woman who does not want to be caught short. Her parents lived through the Great Depression and she heard their stories of not having enough. She has also heard about little old ladies having to eat cat food to survive because of a total dependence on their Social Security benefits. If she takes the advice of the experts and takes a conservative 3.5% of the invested portfolio, the annual fixed payout would be $16,100 ($460,000 × 0.035) After tax of approximately 15%, the net would be $13,685 ($16,100 × [1 − 0.15]). Many people forget the very important fact that proceeds from taxable portfolios may be taxed as regular income, and withdrawals from tax-deferred ones may also be taxable. You must use the smaller after-tax income number to match up against your expenses for budget planning. You must use the larger pre-tax number for the annual withdrawals from your portfolio for investment management.

Jonathan Clements from the *Wall Street Journal* in 2004 considered very low withdrawal rates to be an overreaction to the bear market in 2001 to 2003, and suggested using a 5% or 6% rate but "don't bank on automatically increasing withdrawals along with inflation. Instead, be prepared to slash your spending, if the market turns on you." The idea is to lower your fixed costs so you can have the financial flexibility to lower expenses if you need to. He suggested reducing and avoiding debt and downsizing to a smaller house with less upkeep as two ways to reduce fixed expenses.

Adding Social Security to her income from the previous calculations, Nancy's total picture looks like this:

## FULL RETIREMENT INCOME STATEMENT

**Calculation with Full Benefits, and a Conservative
3.5% Portfolio Annual Withdrawal**

| | |
|---|---:|
| Full Social Security | $16,260 |
| Interest and dividends | $8,600 |
| Rental profits | $2,300 |
| Total Projected Income | $27,160 |
| Less total income taxes | ($627) |
| Net spendable income | $26,523 |
| Less portfolio withdrawal at 3.5% | $13,685 |
| **Total Income*** | **$40,208** |
| **Less Total Expenses**** | **($40,932)** |
| **Net Annual Deficit** | **($724)** |

\* *$3,350 a month.*

\*\* *A rough estimate from chapter 5.*

Nancy is indeed a very fortunate woman. Her income covers almost all her projected expenses at a relatively low withdrawal rate. If she adjusted her withdrawal rate upward slightly to a still conservative 3.65% rate, she has virtually no chance of having her portfolio run out in thirty years, or age 96 following the Trinity Study data. In addition, Nancy would still own her home and twin home investment, which she can use to cover future health care expenses, miscalculations in either her income or expenses projections, or leave as an inheritance for her daughter, two grandchildren, and her church.

The Trinity Study was based on time series historical data calculations and, as discussed, has its flaws. The alternative method was the more dynamic Monte Carlo simulation models such as the one provided free by T. Rowe Price and by other financial advisors. It is based on probabilities, also called levels of confidence, and non–time series based data. T. Rowe Price's model uses a variety of investment mixes in 500 simulated scenarios of how the securities markets could perform in the future. The scenarios represent a spectrum of possible performances for these investment mixes. Using T. Rowe Price's Retirement Income Calculator to calculate Nancy's chances of disaster, she is also in good shape. Using her portfolio with approximately 40 percent stocks, 40 percent bonds, and 20 percent cash asset mix, as provided by Morningstar's X-ray analysis, the calculator produced the good news that her intended withdrawal of $1,380 a month or $16,555 a year (and adjusting for 3% inflation thereafter) has better than a 90% chance of surviving thirty years. In fact her withdrawal rate could be increased to 4.08% and still have a 90% confidence level. If she needed be 99% sure, then she would have to reduce her withdrawal rate to 3.36% percent, which actually is not that far from her projected 3.65% need. This model is available for free from T. Rowe Price and is very simple to use. It is a great tool to evaluate your own portfolio for the appropriate withdrawal rate.

## MONTE CARLO SIMULATOR PROVIDES CONFIDENCE LEVELS OF PORTFOLIO SUCCESS AND WITHDRAWAL RATES

**Nancy's 30-Year Plan of Possible Portfolio Withdrawals**

| Confidence Level | Withdrawal Rate | Monthly Withdrawal | Yearly Withdrawal |
|---|---|---|---|
| 99% | 3.36% | $1,288 | $15,456 |
| 90% | 4.08% | $1,564 | $18,768 |
| 80% | 4.44% | $1,702 | $20,424 |
| 70% | 4.68% | $1,794 | $21,528 |
| 60% | 5.04% | $1,932 | $23,184 |
| 50% | 5.16% | $1,978 | $23,736 |

Source: T. Rowe Price Retirement Calculator using Nancy's data.

For Nancy it makes economic sense to wait to collect Social Security benefits until full retirement age of 66. She would receive her full retirement benefit without having it ravaged by the penalties levied by the SSA for earnings during her early retirement. As previously explained, to do otherwise would be a $100,000 mistake. In addition, using the expense and portfolio assessment and planning tools provided, Nancy has reviewed her portfolio holdings and has chosen to withdraw 3.65% from her portfolio, an amount that will meet her needs as well as maintain a good measure of assurance and flexibility that she will not outlive her resources.

# WITHDRAWAL STRATEGY
# TAX-SMART DRAWDOWNS

What assets you tap for your retirement withdrawals are very important because of the possible taxes on them. You want to defer as much of the tax bite as possible for as long as possible. Tax-deferred accounts are great because they allow your earnings and gains to accumulate and compound without taxes. They can grow at a quicker rate because taxes are not taken out along the way. Therefore, if possible it is wise to use assets in your taxable accounts first and then dip into your IRAs and 401(k)s. Roth IRAs have special tax provisions that can benefit your heirs. So if inheritance taxes are a concern to you, use your Roth IRAs last. Both John Waggoner of *Business Week* in its July 29, 2002, issue and Sue Stevens, president of financial advisory firm Stevens Portfolio Design in Deerfield, IL, had the same advice.

## Hierarchy of Tax-Smart
## Withdrawals During Retirement

1. Taxable portfolio: Long-term capital gains taxed at a lower rate. Ordinary income is taxed at a lower rate because of a lower income during retirement.
2. IRAs and 401(k)s: Keep in tax-deferred account as long as possible, including capital gains, ordinary dividends, and interest income.
3. Roth IRAs: Tax-free distributions, tax-free deferral of income, tax-free to heirs.

## Lump-Sum Distributions

According to Hewitt Associates, 33 percent of workers ages 50 to 59 who change their jobs withdraw all of their 401(k) assets in a lump-sum distribution, which results in a huge tax bite and injury to their nest egg. I have changed jobs many times and each time I roll over my assets into another 401(k) plan. Avoid the temptation to access the money and do the same if you're changing jobs.

When you leave an employer for any reason, you may be offered a lump-sum distribution from your retirement plan. Should you take it or leave it? It depends. If you have a defined contribution plan, such as a 401(k) plan, which is fully funded by you and your employer, then you can leave the money invested in the same assets and stay with the plan. If you are unhappy with the investment choices offered to you, you may consider a change. However, if your employer-matched contributions (if any) are not fully vested, then you may have to forfeit some percentage. You "vest" or own the contributions by remaining employed at the company for a set number of years. If you choose to make job switch, make sure that the plan directly transfers your assets to another tax-deferred plan such as an IRA, in order to avoid income taxes on the distribution.

The other kind of retirement plan is a defined benefit plan. These plans do not have a specific asset balance as your 401(k) or IRA has. These plans are a promise by your employer to pay a certain stream of benefits when you qualify. The company may fund its obligations to the plan out of current earnings, or it may owe the plan money because it chooses to use the money for other purposes or it can't fund the plan because of financial difficulties. As of September 2004, the approximately 29,000 private defined benefit pension plans still in existence in the United States had a cumulative unfunded pension liability of $450 billion. The number of plans is dramatically down from 110,000 plans in 1985 to 57,000 in 1995.

Because of the funding uncertainty, it may be a good idea to take a lump-sum distribution. The company will pay you the present value of the benefits that it promises to you, and you can invest it yourself. If you stick with the plan and the company gets into trouble, such as many airlines have, the company may default on its obligations. It is also possible that the governmental pension insuring body, the Pension Benefit Guaranty Corporation (PBGC), may not cover all the benefits promised in the plan. The PBGC, like Social Security, has its own problems. The PBGC ran a $23 billion deficit in 2004 trying to make good on the promises of plans that have defaulted. In the airline and steel industries only 60 percent of pensioners are receiving their full benefits.

The question of whether to get the money out or not should be weighed on a case-by-case basis. If you choose to take a lump sum, you need to roll it over directly into a tax-deferred account to avoid taxes. It also becomes your responsibility to invest the money so it can provide the benefits that the company once promised you.

## PORTFOLIO BALANCING

A topic related to the withdrawal issue is what happens to your portfolio over time with monthly withdrawals and portfolio gains and losses. To maintain your diversification and your acceptable level of risk, your portfolio should have a goal allocation between the asset classes of stocks, bonds, and cash. Approximately 17 percent of 401(k) participants rebalance their portfolios in some way, according to a study by Hewitt Associates. The bucket strategies mentioned have some implicit goals of asset allocation within them in order to create and maintain the buckets. In Nancy's case the Morningstar analysis told her that her allocation was a conservative 43 percent in stocks, 40 percent in bonds, and 17 percent in cash. In addition, it told her how her stocks and bonds were allocated according to bond maturities and market capitalization, respectively. Over time the stocks can become more valuable in a bull market run-up. The percentage allocation in stocks becomes more heavily weighted and the portfolio becomes more risky automatically. Therefore, your portfolio needs to be monitored and rebalanced to maintain its risk profile. In this way, the appreciated stocks in a bull market are trimmed and reinvested in areas that have lagged. It is also a way to force you to cash in part of your bull market earnings so that in the eventual bear market slide you won't give back all the gains.

Vanguard's Investment Counseling & Research group did a 40-year study from 1960 to 2003 on the effects of rebalancing. They found that rebalancing is essential and reduces volatility of a portfolio's returns, but the frequency of rebalancing did not matter (*In The Vanguard*, Autumn 2004, p.11). The Vanguard Study found that the un-rebalanced portfolio did not have lower returns, but it did have a higher variation of return, the highest annual losses, and hence the highest risk. Vanguard suggests monitoring and rebalancing semiannually, annually, or whenever an asset class strays more than 5 percent from the target allocation. In Nancy's case, she rebalances annually when she meets with her financial advisor. Her Morningstar portfolio monitoring service helps her to keep track of her entire portfolio to easily make the rebalancing calculation. She also minimizes her taxes by rebalancing investments in her tax-deferred accounts whenever possible, which otherwise might trigger taxes in her taxable accounts.

If you rebalance in a taxable account, be careful close to year end. Most funds declare dividends and distributions of capital gains at the end of their tax years, and if you buy funds shortly before they make their payment, you will receive those dividends and distributions and be taxed on the income, even though you did not own the fund when that income was earned. The same taxable situation occurs when you buy a stock near the time of an upcoming dividend payment and you have to pay taxes on that dividend received.

# CHAPTER EIGHT

# Which Retirement Investments Are for You?

This chapter describes some of the investment options and sources of income that are particularly attractive to retirees and that are also heavily marketed to retirees. In addition to mutual funds that Morningstar evaluates and monitors for you, there are many investment opportunities and sources of income available.

## CDs AND MONEY MARKET FUNDS

Certificates of Deposit (CDs) and money market accounts have traditionally provided a relatively low return, but they also have a relatively low degree of risk. Because of the low level of interest rates, small changes in rates make a large percentage change in your income. For instance, in early 2005 bank money market rates averaged 1.5%, yet higher rates were readily available if you were willing to do a little homework. Rates of 3.0% were available from several banks, and could be found by checking rates nationally through *www.bankrate.com* and by inquiring at local banks for unadvertised specials. You can get an indication of the best CD rates each Wednesday in the *Wall*

*Street Journal* in the Money & Investing section. A rate difference of 0.5% may not sound like a huge amount, but it is a 33 percent increase at today's low rates.

Bankrate.com rates the strength of the banking institutions with a star system, similar to Morningstar's star system. Bankrate.com also provides an easy way to get the highest rates in the nation on a wide variety of maturities. Banking nationally is easy and convenient with the largest banks. You may use your local bank for checking and a small savings account, but if you have a large money market account or CD investment it pays to make a national search. As long as you invest with a banking institution that is FDIC insured and do not exceed the limit of $100,000, you are covered. If you have joint accounts, you are covered up to $200,000. If the insured bank becomes insolvent, your principal is guaranteed, but earnings while the bank is in receivership are not.

A smart way to own CDs is to ladder your CD investments. Nancy's portfolio held several CDs that matured every year and provided an average rate of 3.25%. If she held only a 1-year maturity CD, her rate would be a low 1.5% to 2%. But because she owned 1, 2, 3, 4, and 5 year CDs, her average is much higher. This method is called laddering. The CDs have increasing longer maturities; by investing long term, you get rates that are progressively higher, which creates a higher average. In this way if rates increase, a portion of your CD portfolio can be redeemed and reinvested at higher rates. If CD rates decline, the income is somewhat protected because the bulk of her CD portfolio is invested at higher rates. Another benefit of laddering is that progressive annual maturities give you the flexibility so you can make withdrawals annually without incurring early withdrawal penalties. The amount not used each year can be reinvested in a higher yielding long-term CD of, say, five years. After several years of investing and reinvesting in this way, all your CDs will be invested at the higher long-term rate CDs, but will be partially available for use each year when they mature.

Do not be afraid to lock in your money for 5-year periods. If you need your funds before the CD matures, the interest penalty that can be mitigated by owning several smaller denominations of CDs. In addition, the penalty for not investing longer term on the chance that you might need the money could cost you thousands of dollars in lost interest over the years.

There are CD look-alikes out there that you should avoid. They are frequently advertised in the newspaper and on news radio stations. They offer outrageously attractive yields of 9% when banks are paying 3% for similar maturities. These issuers are not banks and what they offer are not CDs. They are unsecured debt securities that are *not* backed by the FDIC. If the yield is too good to be true, there is a reason. For instance, financially troubled companies' bonds pay more interest as a risk premium on their bonds. There is always a reason.

## BOND INVESTMENTS—TIPS

Treasury Inflation Protected Securities (TIPS) are a recent addition to the investments available to retirees. The federal government has issued approximately $220 billion since 1997. TIPS have their principal amount adjusted upward semi annually to match the increases in the Consumer Price Index (CPI). This is a unique investment because of the ability to be able to preserve your real purchasing power over time. So if you hold the bonds to maturity, you have assured yourself a real, after-inflation return on your investment. If you hold an ordinary bond, inflation will erode the value of the fixed principal amount payable at maturity, and the interest payments based on that principal will earn less interest. With TIPS your principal increases annually, so you earn more interest. The current value of TIPS bonds, like other bonds, will fluctuate based on the general level of interest rates and changes in inflation. However, if you hold the bonds until maturity, you will not realize those interim changes.

The downside to this investment is that you pay for that inflation protection with a lower nominal interest rate. In September 2004, the TIPS rates were a real fixed rate 1.8% on a 10-year bond and 2.2% rate on the 30-year issue. The comparable ordinary U.S. government 10-year bond carried a rate of 4% and the 30-year bond had a rate of 5% and both were not indexed for inflation. One of the most valuable features of Social Security benefits is that the benefits are indexed for inflation, just like these TIPS.

Christopher Farrell's article "Why TIPS Are Still a Buy" in the September 2004 issue of *Business Week* said that TIPS were a good addition to a diversified portfolio because they have been one third less volatile than regular Treasury securities of comparable maturity. In addition, TIPS have moved in the opposite direction of stocks, when compared to the S&P 500 or the Lehman U.S. Aggregate Bond Index. Adding investments such as these that are negatively correlated makes a portfolio less volatile. According to Farrell, "TIPS still rank among the safest long-term investments. So don't be fooled—or worried— by price fluctuations. If there is even a remote chance that inflation will stir, you should consider TIPS as a core holding."

To evaluate the attractiveness of TIPS, subtract the TIPS yield from the corresponding conventional Treasury bond. The difference is what called the break-even inflation rate. If the inflation rate exceeds that rate difference during the bond's life, you are ahead by owning a TIPS bond. In September 2004, the 10-year T-Note yielded 4% and the 10-year TIPS yielded 1.8%. The difference of 2.2% (4% − 1.8%) is the break-even inflation rate for the 10-year TIPS bond to beat over the next decade. The financial markets transmit their opinion through asset pricing. The break-even inflation rate of 2.2% in September 2004 was the market's estimation for the rate of inflation for the next decade. In November 2004 the difference widened to 2.5%, which reflected the concern among money managers that inflation would rise faster in the coming decade.

However, there are tax implications to TIPS. They belong in tax-deferred accounts such as IRAs and 401(k)s because the semi-annual increases in principal are taxable, even though you do not receive it until the bond reaches maturity. If you own TIPS in a mutual fund, the law requires the fund to distribute the increase of principal to investors each year so they can pay their taxes. Nevertheless, TIPS are a good way to protect your savings from inflation.

> Owning bonds in a mutual fund means that you never actually own an individual bond to maturity. Therefore, you are always vulnerable to changes in current bond values when you liquidate the asset, even if you have owned a bond mutual fund for 100 years.

## EXCHANGE TRADED FUNDS (ETFs)

Exchange traded funds (ETFs) are increasingly popular alternatives to traditional mutual funds. An ETF is a basket of stocks that is bought and sold on a stock exchange as if it were a single stock. The basket is not composed of an actively managed portfolio of stocks, rather it is composed of stocks of an index. All the major indexes have ETFs based on them, including the Dow Jones Industrial Average. There are ETFs that track industry, country, and even TIPS bond indexes.

Instead of a mutual fund that you can only purchase at the end of the day's net asset value, ETFs are priced throughout the trading day and traded like stocks. When you buy an ETF, you must pay a brokerage fee; however, they are relatively small for larger purchases.

Because ETFs are required to make very few capital gain distributions, ETFs are very tax efficient for investors. In 2001 the average a index mutual fund paid 5.9 percent of its assets in taxable capital gain distributions, while ETFs paid only 0.3 percent of their assets as distributions. Therefore, if you are holding an ETF in a taxable account, your annual tax bill is much less. In addition, management fees are very low, similar to other index mutual funds. Because of ETFs' efficiencies and ability to track broad indexes, they can be a very prudent part of a balanced and diversified portfolio.

## EXCHANGE TRADED FUND TYPES

| ETF Type | Definition | Index Tracked |
|---|---|---|
| DIAMONDs | Diamonds Trust Series | Dow Jones Industrial Average |
| FITRs | Fixed income exchange traded securities | Various Treasuries (including 1-, 2-, 5- and 10-year) |
| HOLDRs | Holding company depository receipts (marketed by Merrill Lynch) | Narrow industry groups (each initially owns 20 stocks) |
| iShares | Index shares | Group of ETFs marketed by Barclays Global Investors |
| QUBEs | Nasdaq-100 tracking stock (QQQ) | Nasdaq-100 index |
| Spiders | Standard & Poor's Depository Receipts (SPDRs) | Track a variety of Standard & Poor's indexes |

| StreetTracks | StreetTracks—State Street Global Advisor ETFs | Various indexes, including Dow Jones–style indexes and Wilshire indexes |
| VIPERs | Vanguard Index Participation Receipts | Several Vanguard index funds |

## FIXED ANNUITIES

The greater your odds of living a long life, the more attractive annuities look. Annuities are as old as time and economists say they are vastly underused for retirement savings. In ancient Rome, *annua* were sold that promised a stream of cash payments in return for an up-front payment. There are several investment products available that provide a fixed lifetime income stream for a fixed payment. Vanguard calls its product an Immediate Income Annuity and is part of its Lifetime Income Program. TIAA-CREF, the teachers' focused mutual fund group, calls its product a Single Premium Immediate Annuity (SPIA). Metlife calls its product an Income Annuity.

Generally, fixed annuities are not well known nor are they aggressively sold by agents. "I can't offer you chocolate chip mint if you don't know what ice cream is," says Beth Hirshhorn, chief marketing officer for Metlife (*WSJ*, David Wessel, "How Not to Outlive Your Savings," 9/30/04, p. D1). Approximately $5.3 billion was invested in fixed annuities in 2004. This relatively small dollar amount shows that annuities are not well marketed. Also, financial professionals make more money by managing money and by earning annual fees than by locking a client's money in an annuity for a one-time up-front commission.

Since most people do not have a pension plan that lasts a lifetime, an annuity is a way to buy a lifelong income. Instead of depending on your employer's ability to pay into the company pension fund, you are counting on the insurance companies that back the annuities. Vanguard's annuities are provided by AIG Life Insurance Company and TIAA-CREF is backed by its own captive insurance company called TIAA-CREF Life. Insurance companies can afford to issue annuities because they invest a retiree's initial premium in a variety of investments. The return on these investments not only provides the income payments they promised to the retiree, but it also creates a profit. Insurance companies reduce their risks by pooling long-lived and short-lived individuals.

Rating agencies such as A.M. Best (*www.ambest.com*), Fitch (*www.fitchratings.com*), Moody's (*www.moodys.com*) and Standard & Poor's (*www.standardpoor.com*) evaluate insurance companies' past performance and current ability to meet their financial obligations. If you choose to invest in an annuity, you must do your homework because there is a real risk if the issuing company defaults. Although annuities are a conservative investment, they should be a part of a balanced portfolio. Putting all your eggs in one basket, even a conservative one, is a very risky move. By allocating a part of your retirement portfolio to fixed annuities, you are linking a portion of your financial security to the credit worthiness of the issuing company. However, annuities that are issued by a financially strong insurance company can be a good alternative to traditional stock, bond, and cash investments. Fixed annuities are illiquid; they cannot be cashed out; and they leave nothing for your heirs if you live past any guarantee option. If you are married you can buy a fixed annuity that will continue for the life of the couple. In addition there is an annuity option for a guaranteed minimum payout in case you die very young. In that case the remainder of the minimum payout would be paid to your heirs. Both annuity options provide a slightly lower monthly payment than a fixed annuity.

Inflationary fears can be addressed by another type of fixed annuity that provides graded payments that increase by a fixed percentage of 1 to 5 percent every year. Initially, the payments would be less per month to compensate for the higher potential income stream if you live a long life. You need to calculate the breakeven on buying inflation-adjusted payments instead of buying a higher initial income stream. You must also take into account that over your life span, a fixed annuity's purchasing power will be eroded over time.

The following chart shows the income stream that a $100,000 fixed annuity provides:

| VANGUARD INCOME FIXED ANNUITY | | |
|---|---|---|
| **$100,000 Initial Investment, Quoted October 2004** | | |
| Purchaser's Sex and Initial Age | Monthly Payout | Monthly Payout 10-Year Guarantee |
| **Males** | | |
| Age 60 | $591 | $579 |
| Age 65 | $661 | $636 |
| Age 70 | $745 | $693 |
| Age 75 | $895 | $779 |
| **Females** | | |
| Age 60 | $558 | $551 |
| Age 65 | $616 | $602 |
| Age 70 | $685 | $656 |
| Age 75 | $817 | $746 |
| **Couple with Joint Survivorship** | | |
| Age 60 | $506 | $505 |
| Age 65 | $557 | $546 |
| Age 70 | $592 | $589 |
| Age 75 | $682 | $670 |

The portion of your annuity payment that is considered a return of your initial investment is not taxable if it is funded outside an IRA or 401(k). The portion attributed to earnings is taxable. There are specific laws that govern this calculation. Generally, the principal is divided over the actuarially average life span of the investor with the remainder of the monthly payment attributed to earnings. The income is treated as ordinary income, not as capital gains. If the annuity is purchased within a tax-deferred account, the entire payment is taxed as ordinary income when the money is withdrawn from the retirement account.

Annuity payments are based on current interest rates. In a period of rising rates, many advisors suggest purchasing annuities on a staggered basis in order to take advantage of those rates. If your savings are invested all at once in an annuity, you are locked into the current rates for the rest of your life.

Here are some alternatives to consider. Vanguard Single 5 lets you lock in a competitive rate for the first five years (3.4% as of 10/1/04), then gives you the option to lock in for another five years, or to reset annually. As the Baby Boomers retire, the demand for fixed annuities will increase and so will the competition to create new products with more choices.

Prudential Insurance's Prudential Retirement developed a new annuity product in 2004 that serves as a bridge for retirees who want to wait for late Social Security benefits at age 70. This product makes sense for those people who estimate a long life and who want to maximize their Social Security benefits. Unlike a vanilla fixed annuity that guarantees an income stream for life, this new annuity guarantees a specific income for a defined period of time. The product is only available to Prudential plan participants, but if popular it may become more widely available (*Investment News,* Liz Skinner, "Prudential Creates Income Bridge to Help Retirees," 11/15/04, p. 20).

## VARIABLE ANNUITIES

What about "variable annuities?" You may have heard of them. Many investment seminars are organized to steer seniors into them. Variable annuities are similar to fixed annuities, but their payout is based on the market performance of the mutual fund that is contained in the investment. There is often a life insurance feature included.

Unfortunately, variable annuities are notorious for their high costs and harsh tax treatment. Salesmen charge high commissions up-front, and on average annual fees are one third more than those charged for a comparable mutual fund (Vanguard and TIAA-CREF being the major exceptions). In addition, there are surrender charges if you cash out early. It is a sure sign of a problem when your advisor recommends these for your tax-deferred accounts. In a tax-deferred account, the tax-favored treatment of an annuity is redundant because it is already tax-deferred. Only in rare cases, where all tax-deferred accounts have been maxed out, do variable annuities make any sense. If you are near or in retirement it makes no sense at all (Jonathan Clements, "Defending a Much Maligned Investment," *Wall Street Journal*, 10/20/04, p. DI).

Even worse than owning a variable annuity, is the salesman who wants you to switch from your current variable annuity to another. In that case you will pay another up front sales charge and higher annual fees! *Forbes*'s Carrie Coolidge had two pieces of advice. "Don't buy a variable annuity. Second piece: If you already have one, don't switch it for another model without researching the costs" (*Forbes*, 11/29/04, "No Surrender," p. 92).

## REVERSE MORTGAGES

Nancy owns her own home and has built up considerable equity over the years. She can tap the equity in her home through a reverse mortgage, and receive a monthly payment.

| NANCY'S HOME EQUITY | |
| --- | ---: |
| 3-Bedroom Home in Montgomery County, Pennsylvania | $220,000 |
| Mortgage on Home | ($35,000) |
| Net Equity in Home | $185,000 |

Fortunately, Nancy has also built up a considerable portfolio to finance her retirement, and doesn't need to sell her home. However, if her portfolio takes an ugly turn for the worse despite all the smart planning she has done, she may have to use the equity in her home. One way to use the equity in your home without having to move is called a reverse mortgage. An AARP brochure calls it "home made money."

A reverse mortgage is a loan against your house that you do not have to pay back as long as you or any co-owners permanently live there, or until you sell your home or declare bankruptcy. You are still required to maintain your property, and pay the taxes and home insurance, just as you would with a conventional loan.

These loans are specially designed for retirees who are homeowners, 62 years and older, and live in their home as a principal residence. Vacation homes do not qualify. The loan is primarily for those with single-family homes, but some multi-unit homes do qualify. There are no income qualifications because you are not obligated to make a monthly repayment. As you take your reverse mortgage cash payments from the bank, the equity in your property decreases and your reverse mortgage debt increases. During your working years you built equity in your home by paying down your mortgage. During your retirement years you reverse the process and take equity out of your home.

The exception to this decline in home equity occurs when property values rise quicker than your payout. Many retirees in the late 1990s and early 2000s who lived in California or the Northeast enjoyed this phenomenon.

The total amount you can borrow is determined by the equity in your home and your age. The more home equity you have and the older you are, the more money you can borrow. Older people can borrow more because their shorter life span means a shorter-term loan, and that reduces the uncertainty for the lender.

The most popular reverse mortgage is called the Home Equity Conversion Mortgage (HECM). It is the only reverse mortgage that is insured by the federal government. The rates are lower because of the federal guarantee, and the terms and fees of the loans are regulated across all the banks that originate the loans. With an HECM you can receive your reverse mortgage loan check all at once in a lump sum, as a monthly check, or as a credit line to tap when you want or need the money. This flexibility is not always available with other reverse mortgages. An HECM is unique because it allows you to choose an annually adjustable rate or a monthly adjustable rate with specific interest rate caps to help protect you from runaway interest rates during a period of high inflation. In order to apply for an HECM you must first discuss the loan with a loan counselor employed by an agency that's approved by the Department of Housing and Urban Development (HUD). You can find a counselor at HUD's listing of approved counseling agencies at *www.hud.gov/offices/hsg/sfh/hecm/hecmlist.cfm* or 800-569-4287 or AARP's Web site listing of AARP Foundation Network Counselors at *www.hecmresources.org/network.cfm*.

An HECM is a good deal when compared to other reverse

mortgages because it usually allows the largest loan advances against your equity, and offers more options to receive your cash payments. To see what amount you may qualify for check the reverse mortgage calculator at AARP's website at *www .aarp.org/revmort.* The loan limits are approximately $160,000 for rural homes and $290,000 for homes in metropolitan areas. Nancy would qualify for a loan equal to the entire $185,000 of equity in her home. The proceeds can be used for any purpose.

Some local and state governments offer reverse mortgages called Deferred Payment Loans (DPLs) and Property Tax Deferral (PTD) loans. Generally, these reverse mortgages have low fees and low interest rates. They are only available to low- or moderate-income applicants, and have restrictions on their use. Typically, the funds are restricted to a single use such as home repairs or property taxes.

All reverse mortgages have costs and fees. They include the appraisal, application fees, origination fees, mortgage insurance premiums (MIPs), and other closing costs similar to those for a conventional mortgage. The fees can be added to your reverse mortgage debt. The total annual cost is called the TALC, and is similar to the fee inclusive APR (Annual Percentage Rate) for other types of loans. It indicates the true total cost of borrowing.

Taxes are always an important issue. The proceeds are not considered income, because they are a loan. However, if you are receiving government assistance such as SSI or Medicaid, the money that you receive from your reverse mortgage could be considered liquid assets that may disqualify you for the low-income benefits.

If you do not own your home outright, the reverse mortgage lender will require that your first mortgage be paid off. Your reverse mortgage can be used to pay off the old mortgage and add it to the balance that will eventually be due on the reverse mortgage. This loan will be paid off when the house is finally sold.

As you receive your reverse loan payments, the debt increases by the amount of the payments, accrued interest, and the initial closing costs. If at the end of the reverse mortgage (when you die or pay it off) the accumulated debt is less than the value of the house, then you or your heirs will get the difference. However, if the debt exceeds the equity value of the home, you are not on the hook for the extra amount. The lender also cannot seek to recover the balance from your other assets or from your heirs. The lender will monitor your debt-to-equity ratio and try to prevent an "overdrawn" situation. This is called the non-recourse limit of the loan.

AARP suggests consulting a trusted advisor to evaluate if a reverse mortgage is good choice for your circumstances. There are con artists that try to sell seniors various goods and then try to induce them to take out a "reverse mortgage loan" to pay for them. No reputable vendor will do that.

Interestingly, AARP also suggests that you consult your heirs before taking a reverse mortgage, because it will affect what will be left to them. It may come as a great surprise to your heirs that the house they expected to get free and clear will be sold by the bank to pay off your reverse mortgage loan. Probably they will support your decision to be self-sufficient, but if they do not, you will have a clear picture of their true motives before you pass on so you can adjust your will accordingly. All adults should have a will, yet 58 percent do not.

## TARGET-DATE MUTUAL FUNDS

You should try to create a retirement portfolio with the right allocation of stocks and bonds; rebalance the portfolio periodically; and choose a more conservative asset allocation as retirement approaches. You can do that yourself or invest in one of the mutual funds that target a specific retirement date. As your retirement date approaches the mutual fund manager moves from a portfolio heavily weighted in stocks to one favoring bonds. Vanguard Group has a group of funds called Target Retirement Funds with funds maturing in 2015, 2025, 2035, and 2045. T. Rowe Price and Fidelity have target-date retirement fund groups with 5-year maturity increments starting in 2010 and ending in 2040. As with any investment, target-date mutual funds should be only a part of your diversified portfolio.

## LIFE INSURANCE

Life insurance is a very important part of many people's financial security. Depending on the value of your portfolio, your needs, and your desire to leave an inheritance to your spouse or children, life insurance may not be necessary. For most retirees their financial obligations to their children and dependents have been fulfilled, so paying insurance premiums may be an unnecessary burden. If you have taken lower cost term insurance there is no residual value, but a whole life policy builds equity. You can borrow against that equity to pay for current retirement expenses. If assets are tight, continuing to pay for life insurance may be a good way to ensure that your spouse will be taken care of after you pass away and Social Security benefits are reduced.

There are other investments that you can make for retirement but the ones included in this chapter include the major categories. *The important thing to remember is you must maintain a diversified portfolio in order to reduce risk, and to monitor your investments regularly.* Your retirement investment and withdrawal plans probably won't be perfect, so be prepared to alter your plan to suit the changes in your situation.

# CHAPTER NINE

# The Future of Social Security: Can You Trust the System and Wait for Benefits?

Your decision to take early Social Security benefits may be influenced by the system's financial health. When I interviewed Nancy, she wondered if Social Security would be there when she was ready to retire. So, even if the economics of the decision tell you to wait, you may opt for early benefits if you feel insecure about Social Security's ability to pay. Your annual Social Security statement tells it to you straight. In September 2004 all Social Security statements sent to everyone said:

*Today there are almost 36 million Americans age 65 or older. Their Social Security retirement benefits are funded by today's workers and their employers who jointly pay Social Security taxes—just as the money they paid into Social Security was used to pay benefits to those who retired before them. Unless action is taken soon to strengthen the system, in just 14 years we will begin paying more benefits than we collect in taxes. Without changes, by 2042 the Social Security Trust Fund will be exhausted. By then, the number of Americans 65 or older is expected to have doubled. There won't be enough younger people working to pay all of the benefits owed to those retiring. At that point, there will be enough money to pay about 73 cents for each dollar of scheduled benefits. We will need to resolve these issues soon to make sure Social Security continues to provide a foundation of protection for future generations as it has done in the past.*

The odds that Social Security will be in default in the next decade are near zero. But there is a real possibility that anyone retiring in 2012 or later will receive reduced benefits. On February 3, 2005, the president made it clear in his State of the Union speech that people 55 or older (those born before 1950) would not be affected by cuts. If you were born after 1950 and are considering early retirement at age 62, you may face reduced benefits.

However, the health of the system should not be the reason you choose early retirement benefits. The fear that your benefits cannot be paid is unfounded. As described in *Money* magazine in November 2004, "the notion that the system is in such bad shape that future retirees might receive little or nothing is totally overblown." In fact, benefits will continue but at 73 percent of the promised level, not at zero, even if the president and Congress do nothing. It is a common misunderstanding, frequently misrepresented in the press, that the current system is a "pay-as-you-go" system. In fact there is a current surplus that began to accumulate in the early 1980s, but it isn't enough to pay for Baby Boomers' retirement. In 2042, the benefits for retirees will have to be paid entirely by those who are still working because the Social Security Trust Fund will be exhausted.

The trustees of the Social Security Trust Fund annually review their current funding and make projections about the future of the Social Security system. The system is composed of several trust funds. The main fund is the one from which retirement and survivors' benefits are paid. It is called the Old Age and Survivors Insurance (OASI) trust fund. The Disability Insurance is paid from the Disability Insurance (DI) trust fund. The two combined are referred to as the OASIDI.

The trustees create three scenarios about the health of the OASIDI trust funds. Their projections look as far as seventy-five years into the future. Alternative I is the "rosy" scenario of a growing economy, low inflation, high worker-to-retiree ratios, high birth rates, and a stable longevity. Alternative II is the "best estimate" because it takes a middle of the road approach. This scenario is commonly reported in the media. Alternative III is the worst case: slow growth, inflation, low birth rates, and many retirees living very long lives.

Using the rosy scenario of Alternative I, there is no financial problem as far as the trustees have projected. Alternative II has the Trust Fund exhausted in 2042. And the worst case, Alternative III, has things going bad in 2030. Surpluses are projected to continue for almost thirteen years. In 2018 the surpluses will end when the Baby Boomers fully load the system with retirees. Then by 2042 the benefits will deplete the Social Security Trust Fund.

The trustees calculate the shortfall over an infinite horizon as $10 trillion dollars. That figure is often cited by politicians, including President Bush, who advocate major reform. Those who advocate more moderate reforms cite the smaller projected shortfall of $3.7 trillion over the next 75 years. The assumptions used by the trustees to project these figures are very conservative. They use a 1.7% annual growth in the economy, yet in the past five years we have experienced a 3% growth rate. Other assumptions include fertility rates, life expectancies, and immigration. The 1997 trustees' report projected the Social Security system's insolvency to occur in 2029. Their 2004 report shows the date of insolvency to be 2042. That's a 13-year change in just seven years without any change in funding! The Congressional Budget Office, using its own set of assumptions, projects the first shortfall in 2052, not 2042. That's why skeptics don't feel there is a crisis, but agree that there is a funding problem that needs to be addressed. Many feel that the hyped crisis is just a way to get the privatization of Social Security passed. Democratic Senator Edward Kennedy, champion of the liberal cause, is a skeptic. He sees sinister intentions behind the push to "fix" Social Security. He believes the "crisis" is overstated by President Bush in order to put in place a conservative agenda. "They did it on Iraq, and they are doing it now on Social Security," says Kennedy.

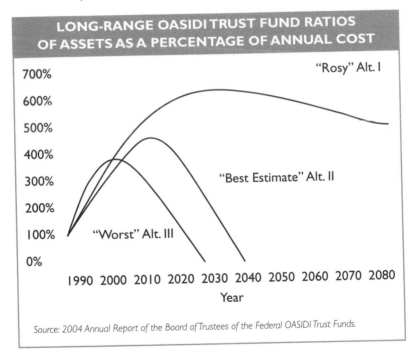

**LONG-RANGE OASIDI TRUST FUND RATIOS OF ASSETS AS A PERCENTAGE OF ANNUAL COST**

Source: 2004 Annual Report of the Board of Trustees of the Federal OASIDI Trust Funds.

The American Council of Life Insurance found in its survey "that more than half the public lacks confidence in Social Security. Nearly two thirds of those younger than 55 have little confidence that they can depend on Social Security being there when they retire." It makes sense that the insurance industry would like to feed that belief. After all, they make their livelihood selling insurance products and annuities to people fearing that Social Security will leave them high and dry.

Social Security currently is running a surplus and has for years. The funds that are not used for current benefits are being used to purchase special U.S. government bonds and the Federal government is spending it for current government expenditures. It is called deficit spending. In return the government is creating government bonds that are owned by the Social Security Trust Fund. Those bonds, like other bonds issued by the Treasury, are backed by the full faith and credit of the United States government so the trust fund is not a "myth." If you cannot put your faith in Treasury securities, you should be investing your nest egg only in precious metals and commodities, not paper money. If our government defaults, commodities will be the only valuable asset. Real estate would not be a good investment because nobody could afford a mortgage and the financial system would be in chaos.

There is a kernel of truth to the myth of the Social Security Trust Fund. It is not a traditional trust fund or endowment that owns private-sector assets. Instead it owns U.S. Treasury bonds. President Clinton's fiscal 2000 budget explained it this way: "They do not consist of real economic assets that can be drawn down in the future to fund benefits. Instead, they are claims on the Treasury that, when redeemed, will have to be financed by raising taxes, borrowing from the public, or reducing benefits or other expenditures" (*Wall Street Journal*, "AARP's Tax Increase," 1/5/05, p. A11). If there had been no Social Security Trust Fund, the *explicit* national debt, which is the amount owed to individual Treasury bond holders, would be far greater. Instead we have a larger *implicit* debt owed to the trust fund and future retirees that is off the books. The actual annual Federal budget deficit is much higher than reported because it includes the annual surplus of Social Security taxes collected over benefits paid. In 2004 Social Security taxes collected but not paid in benefits subsidized $152 billion of deficit spending by the president and Congress. Accordingly the explicit national debt owed to bond holders does not include the government's obligation to the Social Security Trust Fund and therefore it is understated as well.

David Wessel's "Keeping Pension Promise Poses Challenge" in the *Wall Street Journal*, September 16, 2004, explained that "the U.S. is enjoying what has been dubbed a 'demographic summer' in which the large baby-boom generation born between 1946 and 1964 supports the smaller Depression-era generation—for now. In 1960, there were 5.1 taxpaying workers per Social Security beneficiary. Today, there are 3.3." In 2033, there will be 2.1 workers supporting each retiree.

Wessel's outlook is pragmatic. He says

*We will find some combination of restraining benefits, raising taxes, lifting the retirement age, encouraging more private savings, welcoming young immigrants and spurring economic growth (so the pie is bigger when retired baby boomers take their retirement slice.)*

In contrast, Federal Reserve Chairman Alan Greenspan set a gloomy tone at a central bankers' meeting in August 2004 in Jackson Hole, Wyoming. He warned that the U.S. may have already "promised more than our economy has the ability to deliver to retirees" in Social Security and Medicare benefits. He urged policy makers to "recalibrate" benefits without raising taxes. "If we delay, the adjustments could be abrupt and painful. We should recalibrate our public programs so that pending retirees have time to adjust through other channels." Although his suggestions did not alter his own plans to retire on his 80th birthday, he suggested that Social Security be made less attractive by extending the retirement ages beyond 62 for early retirement and beyond 67 for full retirement.

During his second term, President Bush made Social Security reform a top priority. If you were born after 1949, look for some combination of reduction of benefits, payroll tax increases, means testing, an increase in the retirement age, an increase in the early retirement age, and a decrease in the annual cost-of-living adjustments. It is clearly written at the Social Security Web site. Many reform plans, including those put forth by the President's Commission to Strengthen Social Security, preserve scheduled benefits, including cost-of-living increases, for "near retirees." Depending on the proposal, a near retiree is defined as someone aged 55 and older.

In 1983 near retirees were excluded from the changes in retirement age that made the system temporarily solvent. At the time Reagan was president and Alan Greenspan was the Social Security Reform Commission Chairman. The phased-in increase in the full retirement age from age 65 to age 67 is now starting to take effect. According to a 2004 survey by the Employee Benefit Research Institute, only 15 percent of workers 25 through 54 know the age at which they can collect their full retirement. A larger, but still woefully low, 42 percent of workers 55 of age and older know their full retirement age.

Making Social Security solvent may seem impossible, but small changes in the payroll tax rate would close the gap. The Advisory Council on Social Security estimated that a 0.9% increase for workers and a corresponding 0.9% increase for the employer's match would be enough to make this entire problem go away.

Yet, President George W. Bush said in a speech on December 14, 2004, that for the time being payroll tax increases are off the table. "We will not raise payroll taxes to solve this problem." On February 3, 2005, in his State of the Union Address he reiterated his opposition to payroll tax increases. The Social Security problem is far from being impossible to solve. In fact there is more than one possible solution.

## TWELVE PROPOSALS TO FIX
## THE SOCIAL SECURITY SYSTEM

1. Increase the payroll tax for employees and/or employers.
2. Raise the age of full retirement on a mandatory schedule based on an increased measure of longevity.
3. Raise the early retirement age to save money based on an increased measure of longevity.
4. Raise the maximum income subject to Social Security taxes ($90,000 in 2005) to keep up with annual income gains of "high-income workers." Currently a much smaller inflationary annual increase is used. (In 1983 10 percent of total wages escaped Social Security taxes because of the maximum; today 15 percent of wages escape Social Security taxes.)
5. Reduce the annual cost-of-living adjustment (COLA) by aligning the basis of the adjustment to a measure that better reflects the inflation rate than the CPI. Some experts believe that the CPI overstates the inflation experienced by retirees.
6. Extend mandatory coverage to all new state and local government employees, to increase the number of workers supporting retirees.
7. Invest a portion of the Social Security Trust Fund in the stock and bond markets to earn higher returns. President Clinton proposed this idea during a time when the Federal government was running a budget surplus, but Congress did not act upon it.
8. Increase the number of years used in the computation of benefits from the best 35 years to 38 or 40 years. By this calculation many people will have $0 income years, so their benefits would be lower.
9. Tax Social Security benefits like private pension benefits, so that any benefits in excess of your contribution would be

taxable. Currently only higher income retirees pay taxes on their Social Security benefits, as explained in chapter 4.

10. Change the way initial benefits are calculated from a wage-based index to a price-based index. Initial benefits are calculated by using your earnings record and indexing it to a current figure at age 60 in a calculation the SSA calls Average Indexed Monthly Earnings (AIME).

This powerful wage calculation has allowed retirees to take advantage of overall economic productivity, not just price inflation, causing benefits to grow faster than prices. Benefits keep getting larger for each subsequent group of retiring workers. Therefore, two workers who earn identical amounts and pay identical taxes will get different benefit even if they are five years apart in age.

Susan Lee's "The Dismal Science," *Wall Street Journal,* November 13, 2004, explains "using the existing system, the purchasing power of benefits paid to today's teenager are scheduled to be 60% higher than benefits paid to a typical worker who retired in 2001. By using the price index instead of a wage index, workers with identical wages would receive the same real benefit, regardless of age difference. A reduction in an increase is not a cut, and real benefits would be just as generous tomorrow as they are today." For today's youngest workers this change would cut benefits about 40 percent from the levels promised under current law, and that difference would continue to grow as long as the gap between wage and price inflation continues. According to AARP, if such a change had been made in the 1960s, the average senior today would receive a check for $300 instead of the $955 that is the current average. It should be noted that AARP opposes changing the indexes.

This change could make a huge difference over an extended period of time. And since the experts understand its potential it may just fly under the radar and become law. This single change is estimated to make the system solvent, but the retiree less solvent.

11. Means test benefits, so those recipients with incomes or assets above a certain level will have their benefits dramatically reduced or eliminated.

12. Pay different benefits based on gender. Private insurance companies charge women less than men for their life insurance policies because women on average live longer than men. Because of their extended life span, women would pay more premiums over time to the insurance companies to fund their death benefit. Using the same logic, Republican Congressman Bill Thomas, head of the Ways and Means Committee in charge of Social Security, proposed that women receive smaller monthly benefits because their longer life spans will give them more total benefits. He proposed this idea along with those already listed, as one of many ways to address the long-term shortfall in funding.

AARP reviewed the proposals in January 2005 and created a menu of "adjustments" it would consider to cover the projected $3.7 trillion shortfall over the next 75 years. It also calculated the percentage of the shortfall that its favored solutions would cover:

| THE AARP's MENU FOR SOLVENCY | |
|---|---|
| Option | % of Shortfall Covered |
| Raise the cap on taxable wages from $90,000 to $140,000 | 43% |
| Raise retirement age gradually to 70 by 2083 | 38% |

| | |
|---|---|
| Reduce starting benefits to reflect longer life spans | 25% |
| Increase payroll taxes one-quarter of a percentage point, for both employees and employers | 24% |
| Change initial benefits calculation to include 38 years instead of 35 years | 16% |
| Invest 15 percent of trust fund in stocks and bonds index funds | 15% |
| Modify the COLA formula to reduce benefit increases | 14% |
| Require new state and local government employees to join the Social Security System | 9% |

*Source: AARP, as reported in Wall Street Journal, 1/21/05, by Jackie Calmes, "On Social Security: It's Bush vs. AARP," p. A4 (All the options above, if implemented, cover 185% of the shortfall.)*

## REFORM PLANS PROPOSED

There are several formal plans that have been set forth. The Ball Plan, named after Democrat Robert Ball, proposes slowing the increase in benefits with a change in the annual COLA, gradually raising the wages subject to Social Security taxes, adding state and local government employees to the system, and slightly raising the payroll tax rate to cover the projected funding shortfall. Ball joined the SSA in 1939 and eventually ran the SSA under Democratic administrations. He was also part of the commission that temporarily resolved the funding crisis in the early 1980s. Under the bipartisan leadership of President Reagan and Democratic Speaker of the House Tip O'Neill, the retirement age was raised to 67 and payroll taxes increased.

In 2001 President Bush's Commission to Strengthen Social Security proposed Plan Two or Model Two, which recommends adopting a new way to calculate initial benefits. (See number ten on my list.) Plan Two also proposed personal retirement accounts that would divert 4 percent of a person's 6.2% payroll tax rate up to $1,000 the first year, with future annual increases of $100. Those choosing a private account would have their guaranteed benefits reduced by the amount their diverted money would have earned in the Social Security Trust Fund. The Fund has implicitly earned 2% above the inflation rate from the government. In the press briefings for the State of the Union Address in February 2005, President Bush's aides shared that Model Two was President Bush's favored plan for personal retirement accounts. The president made it clear in his speech that he was open to the suggestions to cut benefits by changing the calculation of initial benefits, by changing the COLA calculation, and by making upward adjustments of the early and full retirement ages.

## PERSONAL RETIREMENT ACCOUNTS AND PRIVATIZATION

A key element in President Bush's proposal to reform Social Security is the creation of personal investment accounts. A portion of payroll taxes currently used to fund the Social Security system would go to these new accounts. Although personal accounts are part of the debate to reform Social Security they will not make the system solvent. Republican Congressman Bill Thomas, Chairman of the Ways and Means Committee that oversees Social Security, said on January 18, 2004, "personal accounts don't really solve the problem. You still have a problem of the fundamental system and the way it is funded." Thomas didn't endorse private accounts as an end in themselves, but rather as a necessary ingredient of the Social Security bill because President Bush "demands it." So if they are passed into law, they could adversely affect the benefits of retirees in the distant future.

Instead of a pure collective insurance system, which we currently have, individual investment accounts would not only "privatize" a portion of Social Security, but would also reduce the guaranteed government portion. A presidential aide elaborated on February 2, 2005. He said that the amount of the benefit reduction will be what the diverted money would have earned if it had been invested in the Social Security Trust Fund, at a rate of 3% over the rate of inflation. (This is a 1% increase from the original 2% percentage proposed in the Ball Plan in an effort to decrease the cost.) If the investments in a privatized account earn more than that 3% hurdle rate, the owner of the private account would get higher benefits; if not, the owner would get less. "Under White House ground rules for the briefing, reporters weren't allowed to identify the official by name" (*Wall Street Journal*, 2/4/05, p. A5).

Private account holders would control their investment decisions until retirement. Under the current proposal the SSA would then take the total amount the private account earned, subtract what it would have earned in the Trust Fund, and pay the balance to account owners to spend during retirement as they wish. The amount subtracted would be paid in the form of a monthly annuity to provide a minimum monthly benefit that would last a lifetime. If the retiree dies after beginning to collect the annuity, nothing of the private account allocated to the annuity would be left as an inheritance. If investment returns in the account are poor, then the account holder will receive lower benefits as an annuity than those who did not choose a private account, and no extra account balance to spend or leave as an inheritance. Anyone born in 1950 or after will be eligible to start a private account.

| WHO'S ELIGIBLE? | |
|---|---|
| **Birth Year** | **Year Eligible** |
| Before 1950 | Not eligible |
| 1950–1965 | 2009 |
| 1966–1978 | 2010 |
| 1979 and after | 2011 |

Source: White House, Wall Street Journal, 2/4/05, "Private Accounts Win When Invested Well" p. A5.

The switch to a private account is similar to the switch from a company's defined benefit pension plan to a 401(k); the risk of funding the benefits and making investment decisions is transferred from the employer to the employee. In the case of Social Security, a greater burden, a greater risk, and a potential for a better retirement are put into workers' hands.

Current proposals advocate that retirees will have the option to remain with the current system or to join the new privatized system with a portion of their Social Security contributions. As mentioned, 43 percent of full-time employees do not participate in their employer's 401(k) and many who do join avoid stock and bond investments. They invest in the default investment option of low-risk, low-yielding money market accounts. This conservative inclination by the majority of workers is reflected in a restaurant worker's comments from Sioux City, Iowa, as reported in the *Argus Leader*: "Stocks seem like such a risky thing. One person can make a bunch of money and another person can lose it. I guess if I had to invest Social Security money in an account that way, I would. But if I could leave it where it is, I'd be most likely to do that, for right now."

There are a number of unresolved issues with privatized accounts. A single worker's earning record can currently generate multiple streams of retirement income for spouses, ex-spouses, and dependents. In 2004 there were 6.7 million survivors of workers and 4.8 million spouses, ex-spouses, and dependent children of workers collecting Social Security benefits. Under a privatized system those multiple benefits that are currently funded by the Social Security system may not be possible. The current system is a progressive pension, so even if your income is low during your working years, a higher percentage of your salary will be replaced by benefits. If benefits are determined solely by your own contributions, will there be enough money to provide an income for a surviving spouse?

The concept of privatization can be an attractive option for distant retirees. Their payroll taxes are projected to generate benefits from a 1 to 2 percent return on contributions in the Social Security system. If allowed to invest a portion of their payroll tax money, experts believe, future retirees can get a better return in the market—possibly a 5 percent return. The potentially higher returns from a private account are uncertain and have a higher degree of risk.

In the Bush administration's view, this individual account issue is a "values issue." Private accounts promote an "ownership society" where you own your assets and own the risks. There will still be a government-backed safety net, but it will have some very big holes. President Bush's strategic-initiative director Peter Wehner wrote in a leaked private memo to Republican supporters, "If we succeed in reforming Social Security, it will rank as one of the most significant conservative governing achievements ever."

How are the diverted funds that currently fund retirees' benefits going to be replaced? Experts have speculated that the funding gap or "transition cost" may be $1 to $2 trillion. There are many ways to close the funding gap: change payroll taxes, retirement ages, and/or cost-of-living increases, or increase the Federal budget deficit. In that case the Federal government would need to openly issue more debt on the credit markets, which could crowd out private companies that need credit, raise interest rates, and be a negative factor on the economy. On January 11, 2005, Treasury Secretary Snow told a group of Wall Street bond traders that the transition cost would mean borrowing $100 to $150 billion a year over ten years. The participants said that the market could easily absorb those sales, with one bond executive saying, "Mr. Secretary, that's a rounding error."

In January 2005, *Time* conducted a national opinion poll, and found that 47 percent were opposed to private accounts while 44 percent were in favor. When interviewers told respondents the price tag of $1 to $2 trillion and that guaranteed benefits would be reduced, 69 percent opposed private accounts and only 21 percent favored them. AARP, which has 35 million members, ran a newspaper ad campaign against privatization. It opposes any partial privatization proposal that would divert money from the current system into private accounts. An older couple in the ad said, "If we feel like gambling, we'll play the slots."

Glenn Hubbard, the dean of the Columbia Business School, argued in "How Bush's Plan Would Secure Social Security" in *Business Week,* November 29, 2004, that private accounts would be the financially prudent thing to do:

> *As long as future net obligations are reduced by prefunding Social Security benefits through personal accounts, the diversion of a portion of payroll taxes to personal accounts is akin to prepaying your mortgage. If the transition costs are borrowed, the resulting higher* explicit *federal debt (owed to ordinary holders of U.S. Treasury Bonds) in the near term is offset by the lower* implicit *debt (Social Security future obligations) in the longer run. The*

*present value of Social Security's unfunded liabilities is lowered.*

Again, there is more than one way to reduce future net obligations. This could be accomplished by reducing retirees' future benefits by indexing future benefits to increases in price inflation instead of wage inflation, and by raising retirement ages. Any changes should take a realistic view of the Social Security system's real total obligation to current and future retirees. This is something past presidents and Congress have gone to great lengths to avoid.

Powerful forces in the investment community including banks, financial services companies, and insurance companies favor investment accounts. Some critics have called it a feeding frenzy. It would quickly create a growing trillion-dollar pool of new funds to invest in the market, and then manage. Investing and managing those new sums will generate an estimated $940 billion over the next 75 years in brokerage commissions and management fees. In February 2005 several reports tried to minimize the windfall because the fee accounts would be small and would require a great deal of management. For the general market the new influx of money could support or propel stock prices. Or it could drive the bond market down on fear, especially if there are fears that the transition costs will be too high. It could also lead to higher rates and inflation. The results are entirely unknown.

Some of the proposals for private accounts have provisions for the many financially unsophisticated account owners. To ensure that investments will be balanced and diversified, they suggest that the accounts be limited to no-load index funds and U.S. inflation-protected TIPS bonds. President Bush agreed, and said, "People are not going to be allowed to take their own money for their retirement account and take it to Vegas to shoot dice." President Bush's aide elaborated that investors could choose from a menu of stock and bond funds, as well as some "target funds"—funds designed to tailor investment allocations to become more conservative as a person approaches retirement. Critics of restrictions on investments, but proponents of privatization, feel that any restrictions constitute further governmental interference that is contrary to a push for an "ownership society." The possibility of increased rewards goes hand in hand with increased "responsibility."

There are other questions that remain unanswered. Do workers have to irrevocably participate in a private account system when they enter the workforce, or can they decide later? At retirement can retirees take all their money as a lump sum or will they be required to buy an annuity? Can participants withdraw their funds from their accounts for emergencies?

Despite the arguments against privatization, it is an attractive idea to people who have little confidence in the system. "They say that people in college are more likely to believe in UFOs than they are that Social Security is going to be there for them," said South Dakota Republican Senate candidate John Thune. "They see it as money going down a rat hole." He may have a point. A 43-year-old auto worker at a Ford plant concurs, "My plan is to presume I'm getting zero. And anything I do get from it is a benefit and a bonus." Josh Brown, a graduating college senior at Emory University in Atlanta, agrees with that opinion and approves of the new plans, "I want the option of putting part of my Social Security contributions into a private account. I don't even mind if the government regulates where the investments can be made, so long as I do not continue flushing money down the drain funding the pay-as-you-go system we have now."

There is a downside to investment freedom. Some people may not make good choices, and many people will be hurt by a market crash or deflationary cycle. As our history has shown, "there will be an outcry to bail out the losers. And that will mean higher taxes for the rest of us," according to columnist Jonathan Clements of the *Wall Street Journal* in his analysis "What Privatizing Social Security Would Mean," November 24, 2004. This risk of a possible social revolt in a market downturn is not far-fetched because two thirds of seniors rely on Social Security as their main source of income.

The battle over Social Security is part of a bigger battle of ideology. Political scientist Reichley explained it in *The Life of the Parties,* and John Harwood of the *Wall Street Journal* paraphrased in his article "On Social Security, Bush Is Confronting Ideological Divide": "The Republican tradition champions economic growth and using government to foster 'individual, family and community achievement'—even if that makes society less equal. The Democratic tradition celebrates the use of government to foster equality—even if it makes the economy less efficient." As White House aide Pete Wehner said, "Our goal is to provide a path to greater opportunity, more freedom and more control for individuals over their own lives."

## Other Countries' Experiments with Privatization

Daniel Kadlec reported in "Taking the Plunge" *Time,* November 22, 2004, that private retirement accounts have been tried in other countries. In Chile retirement savings accounts have been considered a success. Begun in 1981, the Chilean system is compulsory for everyone who is employed, to invest in only in a handful of conservative, income-oriented investment options. Self-employed workers are not required to contribute.

Jose Pinera, its architect and Chilean Secretary of Labor from 1978 to 1980, describes a system with no payroll tax for employees or employers. Instead, 10 percent of a worker's pretax wages are invested in a personal account that grows tax-free until retirement. Workers can voluntarily contribute an additional 10 percent a month in pre-tax wages. At retirement Chileans have three payout options: leave the money in the account and make monthly withdrawals subject to their life expectancy; purchase an annuity from an insurance company to guarantee a retirement income; or a combination of the two. If the total expected benefits are greater than 70 percent of the worker's most recent wages, he or she can withdraw the surplus in a lump sum.

For Chile's working poor, there is a low "minimum pension" of $136 (U.S.) a month guaranteed by Chilean law. Chile's minimum wage is $207 per month. If the worker has contributed for at least twenty years, and depletes his or her account, then the government makes the minimum pension payments. Those without twenty years of contributions can apply for welfare payments at a lower level. About 50 percent of the Chilean workforce who will retire over the next thirty years will not have saved enough to provide for their own minimum pensions, according to the Chilean government pension regulator.

In Chile private retirement accounts are managed by a variety of competing management companies that are strictly regulated to prevent conflicts of interest. They have funds similar to the Target Retirement funds from Vanguard or T. Rowe Price. The closer investors are to their retirement, the more conservative the investment choice.

In Britain a private account system was started in the late 1980s, but it has not gone very well. Their system gave incentives to convert to private accounts, but it did not put many restrictions on investments. Many unscrupulous advisors put unsophisticated investors in unsuitable, risky investments. Millions who joined the new system in the recent market downturn did worse than they would have with the old pension system.

Other countries have systems with private accounts. Since 2000 Swedes have invested 2.5 percent of their total 18.5% payroll taxes into "premium pension accounts" that are individually controlled. Swedes can choose from 660 funds or pick a default portfolio run by the government. Their initial enthusiasm for managing their own money wore off after the market setbacks in 2001 and 2002. Now all but 8 percent have gone to the more conservative default portfolio run by the government.

Argentina and Bolivia also began private account systems in the 1990s. Both faced larger transition costs than had been projected. Their economies were not strong enough to shoulder their governments' budget deficits along with the large transition costs to private pension systems. As a result these countries defaulted on their national debts and could not pay all of their promised pension benefits.

## NOTHING HAS BEEN PASSED YET!

With any proposal for reform, the Social Security trustees will independently evaluate all the proposals and make projections about possible consequences. Then Congress will have to go along with the president and vote for the reform measures. It is a lengthy process and many special interest groups will chime in before any proposal becomes law. For Nancy and for all those contemplating retirement in the near future, this Social Security debate—however it turns out—will not affect their benefits. The outcome could have a major impact on your investment portfolio, especially if the market dislikes how the plans could negatively impact the economy. An uncertain economy leads investors to demand higher interest rates, which lead to lower corporate profits, which cause a fall in stock prices.

The issue of Medicare is largely being ignored by the government and the media, but it affects Nancy more directly than Social Security. The Social Security problem concerns a solvable $10 trillion long-term unfunded liability (perhaps $3.7 trillion with a shorter 75-year time horizon), while Medicare has a $29 trillion long-term unfunded liability fueled by rising health care costs and a rising number of retirees. Medicare is not a problem that can be fixed by tweaking benefits. It will require deep cuts in care or steep increases in premiums. And because it is not as "easily" solved as Social Security's funding problems, the fire continues to smolder and—surprisingly—is even being stoked. The unfunded prescription drug benefit that begins in 2006 has added $17 trillion of Medicare's long-term funding deficit. By 2030 the trustees project the Medicare Trust Fund will be exhausted without a change in course. But that is an issue to be tackled in another book.

# CHAPTER TEN

# How Do You Apply for Benefits?

Whether you decide to take early Social Security benefits or wait until full retirement, you must apply for your benefits. Neither an application nor a check will be sent to you automatically. It is very important to apply promptly because you may forfeit some benefits if you file late. If you are uncertain about your eligibility, you can protect your filing date by submitting a protective filing statement. You can file an application without prejudice and if you are denied, you have the right to appeal.

If you aren't sure that you'll retire early, you may want to file a protective filing before you become 62 just in case circumstances emerge later in the year that compel you to apply early. There is no protective filing application form provided by the SSA. Just write a letter to the SSA, request your benefits, and sign the letter. If later in that year you decide to file the full application, you can get benefits from the date of the protective filing instead of the date of the application. It is best to mail the application via a method that provides proof of delivery. That way you'll have a receipt if it gets lost in the mail or misplaced at the SSA. The protective filing is effective for six months after the SSA advises you that it received your letter. However, you must file an application within that six-month period. If the six months lapse, you either submit another protective filing, a formal application, or wait. If you file a protective statement at a Social Security office, get a copy of the statement for your records in case it gets lost at the SSA.

*Social Security Administration*
*Office of Central Operations*
*P.O. Box 17775*
*Baltimore, MD 21235-1213*

The rule of thumb is to file a full application three months prior to the month that you intend to retire. There are circumstances whereby you can collect benefits months before you actually retire. This is due to the peculiar nature of the Annual Earnings Test and rules governing retroactive payments. If you earn less than the annual Annual Earnings Test limits during the first year of early retirement ($12,000 in 2005), then it is best to file either an application or a protective filing in January of the year that you might retire.

If early retirement at age 62 is your choice, your first check will be for the first month that you are 62 years of age "throughout the month." It is called the full month rule. For example, if you turn 62 on June 15th, your first month's check will be for July. Since the SSA pays benefits in arrears, you will get your July payment at the beginning of August. If your birthday is on the 1st or 2nd of the month, you are entitled to benefits for that month. For example, if you turn 62 on June 2nd, your first month's check will be for June. Since the SSA pays benefits in arrears, you will get your June payment at the beginning of July.

# MAKING CONTACT
# WITH THE SSA

The first contact that you have with the SSA will probably be with a Service Representative (SR) on its toll-free number: 800-SSA-1213. SRs answer general questions from 7 AM to 7 PM in all time zones. The peak hours are 10 AM to 3 PM so try calling before or after those times to avoid a wait. In addition, try not to call at the beginning of the month because the majority of checks go out then and recipients who have questions and complaints call the SSA at that time. The SR will ask if you would like to file your initial claim in person or by phone. If you choose a phone interview, then the SR will make a telephone appointment for you with a Claims Representative (CR). It will take about two weeks for the appointment. Most people (about 80 percent) choose the phone route. You can also file online at *www.socialsecurity.gov/applytoretire*. The website is fine for only very straightforward cases. The Claims Representatives on the phone are very well trained and can help you obtain benefits that you may not be aware of. This is not a process that you should rush through, and the CRs guidance could be invaluable.

If you choose to go to one of 1,100 district offices across the country to make your claim in person, there is a SSA office locator at *www.ssa.gov*. Since you cannot make an appointment at a district office, and are served on a first-come, first-served basis, go toward the end of the month. It is a less hectic time. Also avoid Mondays, lunchtimes, and office coffee break times at 10 AM and 3 PM.

The person who actually files your application, the Claims Representative, is trained to answer complex questions about filing your claim. In March 2004 an internal study by the SSA showed that CRs gave correct answers 97.8 percent of the time to questions about eligibility and benefits. That is amazing when you consider the complexity and variety of the situations presented to them and the many ways that people may ask their questions or present their circumstances. CRs are not rewarded if they reject your claim, like David Spade's character the "No Man" from Capital One credit cards. On the contrary, the CRs are evaluated on their ability to provide you with the highest possible benefits that you are entitled to. In their jargon you are a "number holder" before your apply; a "claimant" when you apply; and an "appellant" if you are denied benefits and appeal. All the rules, and interpretations of the rules that guide your CR's decision about your benefits, can be found in a book called the Programs Operations Manual System (POMS). It's the Social Security bible.

Your interview will be very cordial, and will last about 20 to 30 minutes. The CR wants to get the required identifying information, your work history, and the date you plan to retire. During the application process you will answer a series of questions, and the CR will use the information to complete your application. These key pieces of information that the SSA needs are listed below:

**Identification:** Name, maiden name, and Social Security number—to prove you are who you say you are

**Age:** Date and place of birth and the substantiating documents to further verify your identity

**Work History:** Your current employer, recent employers, and your earnings histories—so the SSA can update and verify your record since its last report

**Family:** Your spouse, former spouses, children, and dependents—so the CR can determine if you are eligible for payments based on your work record, your spouse's, or even your ex's work record.

**Payment Desires:** Where and how you want to be paid—the

SSA can send a check by mail or deposit funds directly to your bank account. Not only are thousands of checks lost each year, but Social Security's cost to mail a check to you is higher than a direct deposit.

The CR will fill out your application, send it to you for your signature, and ask you to supply certain documents. To verify your age you will have to send your original birth certificate. For your recent wages you need to send your W-2s. To verify your marital status, you may be asked for marriage certificates or divorce decrees. If you are filling out an application in person, take these documents to your initial visit to the SSA office and save yourself a second visit.

The Claims Representative will review your completed application, documentation, and earnings record to determine your eligibility for benefits and any possible retroactive payments. If your application is approved, the CR will send an award letter that outlines your benefits. If your claim is denied, you will be sent a denial letter stating the reasons for the denial.

After you receive a denial letter, all is not lost. You can appeal the decision and become an appellant. Honestly, the SSA is not out to get you. If it has made a mistake, it will gladly correct it. If you are lacking documents or qualifications, the SSA will explain what is needed. If it is a simple matter, you may be able to comply and get a quick approval.

If you are not approved after trying to comply with the requests, you can formally appeal. The first level of appeals is called reconsideration. Your appeal must be in writing on a one-page form and must be submitted within sixty days. At this stage you are able to provide new information or documentation and will have the chance to make your case to a fresh set of eyes. If that does not resolve the problem, you can request a hearing. As a final recourse, there is the Appeals Council Review in Washington, DC, or you can file suit in Federal court. The vast majority of applications are approved at the beginning of the process, and no appeals are necessary.

## YOU MUST APPLY
## FOR MEDICARE

At age 65 you are eligible for Medicare, and like Social Security, you are not automatically enrolled. Interestingly, if you are collecting early Social Security retirement benefits before the age of 65, you are automatically enrolled and the premium is deducted from your Social Security benefits check. However, if you are beginning your Social Security benefits on or after age 65, you must apply for your Medicare coverage. The SSA, which administers both Social Security and Medicare, suggests that you apply three months before your sixty-fifth birthday for Medicare.

If your full retirement age is past 65 because of retirement reforms, you are still eligible for Medicare coverage at age 65, even if you are still working. Many employers' health plans have special rules concerning employees who retire under the age of 65, and rules for employees continuing to work past age 65. You need to check how your employer's health plan affects you. It's important to apply promptly for Medicare or you may be subjected to late Medicare enrollment premium penalties.

In addition to Medicare, there are supplemental policies available by private insurers. Medi-gap policies cover deductibles and other medical expenses. The six-month period after you enroll in Medicare is the only time insurers are required, by law, to provide open enrollment for coverage—even if you have pre-existing medical conditions. After that time, insurers at their discretion can reject your application for coverage.

As illustrated in Nancy's case, the high cost of medical insurance during early retirement is a major factor in choosing whether or not to retire early, but when you are eligible at age 65, whether you work or not, you need to apply.

# CHAPTER ELEVEN

# Prepare and Beware: Are You Prepared to Fend Off Scam Artists?

Near retirees and early retirees are the prime targets for fraud. In the *Wall Street Journal* article titled "Confessions of a Con Man," Eric Stein, an incarcerated con man in Fort Devens Federal Prison Camp in Massachusetts, talked to reporter Glenn Ruffenach. What Stein has to say is eye-opening. "His comments provide an insider's look at swindles that rob Americans of billions of dollars each year—and help explain why adults approaching retirement rank among scam artists' favorite targets."

Stein's victims have similar traits or experiences. If you see yourself fitting his profile, don't be embarrassed, beware. Stein clearly describes his victims and that is why it is so important to listen:

*All [defrauded] investors ultimately have a common characteristic: They're risk takers. [Some] guys—we call them "hard money" or a "mooch"—just like to play it really big. . . . One of the major players that we go after are people close to retirement or have recently retired. They've been hammered in the stock market for the past couple of years, or they've made bad decisions with mutual funds, or whatever.*

Many people feel victimized by the financial markets and all the scandals, such as Enron, WorldCom, Adelphia, ImClone, mutual fund rapid trading, and Arthur Andersen's deceptive accounting practices. A typical pitch preys on this vulnerability and goes like this: "Look, you can't trust corporate America. You should have gotten great returns on a particular stock, [and] you didn't because they are manipulating it. [By contrast] this guy has a general partnership; he's a small-business owner. You can trust him."

"[Near retirees and early retirees] don't have the business opportunities they had when they were younger, and as they get closer to the time when they really want to sit back and relax— so to speak, as the sand passes through the hourglass—they are people that [scams] are hammering the hardest."

The majority of victims are not a bunch of little old ladies; quite the opposite, as Stein describes:

*The majority of clients that I [Stein] dealt with over the years were white-collar types of people. They were people who were already successful. They were people who had cash—had made money— and had worked very hard for it. They were doctors, they were dentists, attorneys, car-dealership owners, golf-course owners, some high-profile restaurateurs. A lot of business owners, mostly entrepreneurs.*

The "openers" or "screeners" make thousands of calls to people whose names appear on lists of contest entrants, mall intercept interviews, survey responders, and timeshare owners. If they get a person who appears to be interested in the opportunity, the opener briefly explains the opportunity and then turns the person over to a "seller." If the "seller" cannot softly complete the sale himself, then the "closer" is brought in to size up the victim's resources, overcome objections, and close the deal. The closers provide references, usually people involved in the scheme or other investors who were given great returns, so they would provide glowing testimonials.

The deals that seem somewhat plausible commonly offer large payoffs, 20 to 25 percent or more every ninety days. As Stein says, "Truth is, 25% on a quarterly basis is impossible—can't happen. But you're not going to believe that it can't happen. Because you want to believe that it can happen, because that's what you want to happen."

Most financial scams begin with a plausible idea from an "issuer." The business plan is usually very clever. It relates to something "current in the marketplace" that people are familiar with, such as cellular spectrum licenses or Stein's scam revolving around direct-response television marketing. This is called a "hook" that leads you into the scam. The issuer goes to a group of professional thieves, called an independent sales group (ISO) that takes the idea and uses it to defraud investors. These ISOs are comprised of people who have typically gone through several cycles of these scams, and know how to get others hooked into the newest get-rich-quick scheme.

## The Seven-Step Scam Spam Filter

Use it for your protection.

1. Never talk to any financial salesperson on the phone whom you do not know personally. No need to be polite, just hang up.
2. If someone sends you an e-mail or brochure in the mail regarding a financial opportunity, ignore it. Throw it out.
3. If you are considering buying stocks or other financial products, buy them only from a licensed and registered broker from a reputable firm that you know. Never buy anything from a "broker" from Canada. Be especially suspect of anything sold unsolicited by a brokerage firm from Florida, Utah, or Idaho.

4. Never purchase "unregistered securities." These do not have to comply with governmental regulations. They do not trade on a national stock exchange, so you cannot sell the investment by simply calling your broker.
5. Avoid private placements, partnerships, and membership units in a limited liability corporation (LLC). There are legitimate opportunities like these, but they are for truly sophisticated investors. They are not sold over the phone and are usually available to people well connected in the financial community. Thieves prey on your desire to get in on such exclusive "opportunities," where all the fat cats have made their easy money.
6. Never buy a financial product that is described as "low-risk, high-yield," or "safe" because a friend, relative, religious leader, or parishioner has recommended the opportunity to you. Keep a wide separation between your church and your investing activities.
7. Never answer any survey or enter a contest or sweepstakes while shopping in a mall or while online. These lists are sold to scam artists. Thieves call them "sucker lists" because people that think they can get something for nothing and believe in being "lucky."

*Source: Adapted from the Wall Street Journal, 8/9/04, p. R1, "Confessions of a Scam Artist," by Glenn Ruffenach and other sources.*

## PONZI SCHEMES

Most of the major frauds, like Stein's, are a variation on a Ponzi scheme. It is an investment scheme in which returns are paid to the early investors entirely out of the money that the new investors pay to get in on a good deal. Ponzi schemes are similar to pyramid schemes; however, Ponzi schemes are operated by a central company. Pyramid schemes involve chain letters that are independently circulated to willing victims. These schemes begin with a plausible business plan that does not work.

The name Ponzi scheme comes from a huge swindle that occurred in 1919 and 1920 that robbed thousands of people of millions of dollars. Charles Ponzi found a small loophole, his hook, in the international postal system. In a business transaction with a Spanish magazine, Ponzi received an international postal reply coupon. The idea behind the coupon is to take it to your local U.S. post office and exchange it for U.S. postage stamps in order to send a business reply back to Spain. Ponzi noticed that the postal coupon was purchased in Spain for Spanish money worth only 1 cent in U.S. dollars, but in the U.S. the post office provided 6 cents worth of stamps to send the reply. In theory, you could buy $1,000 dollars of reply coupons in Spain and convert them into $6,000 in stamps in the U.S. That was the big idea. If you do this with ever-larger amounts, you could parlay it into an immense and ever-growing fortune.

The red tape of dealing with the various postal organizations and the complications of transferring currencies made the Ponzi scheme inoperable. However, the idea was very seductive. At the height of the frenzy, Ponzi took in a million dollars per week at his Boston office. He promised 50% interest in 90 days, and at the beginning he actually paid investors. The news of those investors' initial good fortune spread like wildfire until there weren't enough new investors to pay the returns to the earlier ones. That's when Ponzi's scheme collapsed, and that's how other schemes fall under their own weight.

Stein's scheme involved a direct-response television marketing company. The company would source products, create commercials, buy inexpensive media time in smaller cities, and try to sell the goods. The products ranged from talking pet ID tags to fitness equipment. His company offered investors "media units" costing $5,000 each. The money from the media units was used to purchase TV time. The 200 commercials would sell five products each for a total sale of 1,000 items. The company would pay the investor $7.50 on each product sold. Therefore, every 90 days an investor had $7,500 to look forward to for each $5,000 media unit he had purchased. Unfortunately for investors, the cheap media time does not exist in the volumes necessary to keep this scheme going. Also, it was not always possible to sell five units per airing. Therefore, the sales of $19.95 products could not sustain a $7.50 per unit royalty. It sounded good in theory, but like Ponzi's stamp hook, it could not be practically executed. Some of the money Stein raised was used to actually create commercials, buy some media time, and pay investors so they would be willing to invest more money. The majority of the money was used to support the lavish lifestyles of Stein and his telemarketers. When the amount coming in could not support both the ongoing payments to investors and Stein's lifestyle, the scheme collapsed.

## PENNY STOCK DEALS

In addition to traditional Ponzi schemes, there is another type of fraud involving the stocks of small companies that often ensnares people on the verge of retirement. The movie *Boiler Room* clearly describes stock scams, and it is a Ben Affleck movie that really is worth watching. In this type of scam, small brokerage firms control the securities of a small company that's traded on an over-the-counter exchange such as the Pink Sheets, the OTC bulletin board, or a Canadian exchange. These shares traded at prices below $5, often pennies a share. Seemingly a true bargain opportunity—where investors can buy thousands of shares like Wall Street players, who buy big companies on the New York Stock Exchange. Because they are small companies traded on small exchanges, they are not required to meet listing standards governed by the Securities and Exchange Commission (SEC). And many do not have to file financial reports with the SEC. Without a source of legitimate information, promoters can just make up stories about "outstanding" opportunities.

Since the stock market's recovery in 2003, stock frauds are getting popular again. "When markets are going up, people are more apt to dabble in stocks. So when you receive this information [about a hot company]—no matter where it's coming from—if it's a bull market, you may be more willing to listen to it," said Peter Wysocki, assistant professor at MIT's Sloan School of Management.

The brokerage firms, often located in Boca Raton, Florida, or Vancouver, Canada, have a team of telemarketing brokers who make cold calls to lists of prospects. Mr. Stein had used the same technique. Some firms are located in Idaho or even Aruba. They can be located anywhere. They find prospects by cold-calling the names on the lists. The first call typically provides information about an investment "opportunity," and uses the names of well-known companies to generate interest, to find out about your assets, and to establish a trust relationship. The second call involves a reminder of the previous call, and builds trust without any selling. Then the caller mentions the penny stocks that the brokerage house controls and cites impressive price run-ups, but never any collapses. The third call is the closing call with the confidential tip so you will invest your money in the new hot stock of the day. This "great" tip may be for a company that doesn't have an operating business or even a plan to get into one.

The typical scenario follows a boom and bust cycle. The broker is very eager to have you buy in the "pump-up" phase, but very reluctant to place your sell order to cash in your profits in the broker's "dump" phase. In some cases, brokers refuse to make the sale that you direct. In just about every case these investments end in disaster.

The same process occurs much more efficiently over the Internet. The promoters send out spam e-mails touting the best new company since Microsoft. They create phony research groups and sham brokerage houses. Bogus newsletters tout the stock in impressive faxes, and confederates talk up interest in chat rooms. You can be certain that if you are buying, insiders are selling. For example, I received this spam at my e-mail address *retire.early.question@juno.com*. It is a perfect example of what to avoid. Of course, I have changed the company's name to protect the guilty:

HOT STOCK ALERT
DECEMBER 2004
ISSUE #82.

Company: South Carolina Astro Machine Corp.
Stock Symbol: SCAM
Current Price; $0.20

We recently alerted you to this stock when they it was featured in a full page ad as in INVESTOR'S BUSINESS DAILY. This newsletter is read by almost 720,000 investors worldwide. This is a serious wake-up call, and we expect it will bring huge interest in the investment community. In the stock market, this usually precedes upward momentum in a stock!

Friends, this opportunity does not present itself often, especially at this price level. You can get in on the "ground floor" of this stock. We've just learned some exciting news about South Carolina Astro Machine Corp. ("SCAM") that pertains to it's exciting future in the stock market.

There are many truthful, legitimate small companies that issue low-priced stocks that have made millions for their investors. But the probability of your hearing about them through an unsolicited phone call, e-mail, or fax is as likely as your being hit by lightning.

## CLAIMING PRIZES OR UNLOCKING
## BANK ACCOUNTS

A large number of scams focus on claiming lottery winnings or unlocking distant bank accounts. One goes like this: You have won a lottery and you must deposit money in order to claim the prize. Forget it. You didn't win. In a twist to the same theme, somebody else has won a lottery, but for various reasons cannot claim the millions. That person needs you, yes you! to claim the prize. However, you must make a security deposit as a guarantee that you won't take all the money for yourself and cut out the winner. Silly as it sounds, this scam brings in millions for unscrupulous telemarketers each year. They just keep calling those gullible people who have entered contests and answered surveys.

For some odd reason the country of Nigeria is a den of fraud. The most popular scheme involves e-mails that require your money as a deposit to unlock millions frozen in a bank account of some wealthy soul. This person, and his entire family, have died unexpectedly. The Nigerian requires an American to help him claim the money frozen in the account. Again, in order to get the cash, your money is required as a security deposit. In return the Nigerian will reward you for your help by multiplying your deposit many times over.

Imagine receiving an e-mail from Mr. Frank Nichols that says, "the Central Bank of Nigeria is holding $35 million that rightfully belongs to the estate of Jonathan Swift, who died in a plane crash. However, none of his relatives had shown up to claim the money. If you would work with Mr. Nichols within the next ten days, half of the money can be yours. To protect Mr. Nichols's interests, and to ensure that you will not run off with his entire $35 million, he wants you to deposit some good-faith money in his account." There are no millions, no Nigerian opportunity, and no "Mr. Nichols." If you fall for this pitch you will be wiring your money into a black hole in space.

In another version of this scam "Mr. Nichols" will choose a family name for the victim who died in the plane crash or auto fatality that matches your last name. This twist makes the scheme more believable. Of course, you are the lucky one who holds the key to the millions! And just the other day, Mrs. Suha Arafat, the persecuted wife of the late Yasser Arafat, e-mailed me that she needs my assistance to get $21 million released from a secret bank account for her poor daughter Zahwa. Oh, that's a version of the "wealthy political leader in trouble and needs-your-help" scam. It's equally entertaining.

## MULTI-LEVEL MARKETING

You may consider multi-level marketing (MLM) as an opportunity to supplement your retirement income and a way to strike it rich. The Federal Trade Commission has warned the public that "many multi-level marketing companies that market their products through distributors sell quality goods at competitive prices, but many offer goods that are overpriced, have questionable merits, or are downright unsafe to use."

In addition to selling products, many companies also sell "opportunities." These opportunities are the chance to become a distributor of the product; to sell others on the "opportunity"; and to make an override on their sales and the sales of the distributors they have recruited. In many cases the product involved is merely incidental or a "hook" to make the MLM operation look legitimate.

As a new distributor you are required to make an up-front investment to join. In return you are able to sell the products at a profit, plus earn a commission on all the sales from distributors that you bring on board. The FTC warns: "steer clear of MLM plans that pay commissions for recruiting new distributors."

The FTC cautions, "a distributor may tell you that for the price of a 'start-up kit' of inventory and sales literature—and sometimes a commitment to sell a specific amount of the product or service each month—you'll be on the road to riches. No matter how good the product and how solid an MLM plan may be, expect to invest sweat equity as well as dollars for your investment to pay off."

There are successful and legitimate MLM companies that sell baskets, candles, kitchen gadgets, and soaps, but there are just as many companies that are not legitimate. You cannot rely on personal referrals that a particular MLM is legitimate, because they may have been duped and haven't realized it yet. You are responsible for the claims that you make about the products and business "opportunities" that you sell to others, so be careful. If you recruit friends and relatives into a scam, you could lose a far more valuable asset, your relationships.

Play it safe. Nobody is going to sell you a legitimate get-rich-quick-scheme. There are "opportunities" out there, but you have to create them yourself.

## TIMESHARE "INVESTMENTS"

Although this is not technically a scam, timeshares are just a misguided expense disguised as an investment. Timeshare sales have soared to $9.4 billion worldwide because so many people are listening to the pitch, accepting the incentives, and buying into the "clubs." Since the average buyer is 53 years old and approaching retirement, I have decided to include this segment. The pitch may include a promise of savings, increased value, inflation protection, and the ability to share the asset with your heirs. Salespeople state that prices for timeshare weeks are rising each year and that units are selling out. This implies increased value. It is a very slick pitch that capitalizes on the name of a famous hotel for legitimacy, yet it is a separate division from the hotel operation.

Unlike real estate, a timeshare depreciates dramatically the moment you buy it. It's like a car that depreciates as soon as you drive off the lot. To gauge the value of a timeshare check the timeshare resale prices. Go to websites such as sellmytime sharenow.com. Check with local real estate firms in the resort area you are interested in, and get an idea of the price of timeshare resales. Check eBay for timeshare listings. Get an idea of the depreciation that your potential "investment" can incur if you buy one. Does the timeshare you wish to purchase let you sell the week back to the timeshare marketer? If yes, ask what the repurchase price will be.

A timeshare is not a real estate investment. Real estate has appreciated tremendously in resort locations throughout the country. With a timeshare you own the right to occupy a room, cabin, or suite for a week or more every year. Additionally, you have the privilege to pay a maintenance fee that is about $1,000 per year. If you fail to pay your maintenance fee, you could lose your investment and be sued for unpaid fees.

Are there any real savings to timeshares? Let's take a look. If you want to stay at a very nice hotel at $300 a day, that room would cost $2,100 for a week-long stay the conventional way. For instance, I stay at the Four Seasons Hotel, one of the premier five-star hotels in the world, for two days every year while on business. The room rate is $225 per night. The up-front cost of a week-long timeshare from the Marriott, Hyatt, or Sheraton is about $25,000. With the $25,000 fee you have purchased the right to save $1,100 a year, $2,100 less the annual fee of $1,000. (If you choose to trade your week for a week at another resort, there may be trading fees or membership subscriptions that reduce that savings.) It would take 23 years to break even on the $1,100 savings ($25,000/$1,100), assuming the inflation rate of rooms equals the inflation rate of the maintenance fee.

If the $25,000 timeshare "investment" had been used to purchase a bond, it could have earned income. Conservatively invested in long-term U.S. Treasury bonds that yield 5%, you would earn $1,250, less taxes of 25%; that would have been $938 of income each year. You could have used your bond income to finance part of your vacation, and the $25,000 would still be yours. Instead, the big vacation savings you had expected from the timeshare is just $162 a year ($1,100 − $938). Plus, you are out the $25,000 purchase price! You would break even in 154 years ($25,000/$162)!

There is a silver lining for near retirees and retirees. Since marketers are desperate to sell you a timeshare, they are offering great deals on vacations to their best resort areas to visit their "vacation resorts" or "vacation clubs." The real opportunity here is to visit these resorts on the cheap. Suffer through their 90-minute presentation (relax, you're retired). Enjoy your vacation, but leave your checkbook at home.

## IDENTITY THEFT

The last piece of this anti-fraud section directly relates to your Social Security number. With that single piece of information in hand, a thief can steal your identity, access your money, and steal from others while using your name. Gartner Research estimated that there were 7 million victims of identity theft in 2003. The Identity Theft Resource Center reported that in 2003 the average thief opened eight credit card accounts and charged $92,893 to the victims; and opened checking accounts and wrote seventy-five checks.

Identity theft is one of the most stressful experiences you'll ever have. Your name and credit are dragged through the mud. The good name that you have established over the years is destroyed. It may take months or years of heroic efforts to clean up the mess. The Identity Theft Resource Center estimated it took the average victims 600 hours and $1,495 in expenses to clear their names and reverse the charges.

## Steps to Protect Your Social Security Number

- Shred all personal documents with your Social Security number on them before trashing them.
- Do not print your Social Security number on checks for check cashing purposes.
- Do not carry your Social Security card in your wallet or purse.
- Do not have your Social Security number written on anything in your address book, résumé, Palm Pilot, or computer.
- Do not provide your number to others unless absolutely necessary. Many forms ask for the number, but leave it blank unless absolutely required to give it.

Beware of an Internet scam called "phishing." Information thieves will send you an e-mail or pop-up message to deceive you into disclosing your credit card numbers, account numbers, passwords, and Social Security number. They often pose as legitimate businesses that you deal with, such as banks, eBay, credit card companies, credit bureaus, or even your Internet provider. The message uses graphics and logos exactly like the real ones. These messages will ask you to "update" or "validate" your account information quickly or else you will have some dire consequences. They will say that there has been a security breech with your account, when in fact the security breech will occur if you respond to their message.

You can protect yourself. Ignore any request from an e-mail

or pop-up message requesting your personal information, especially your Social Security number. These messages have "links" within them to the thieves' websites so they can gather the information. Never click on them. Think about it: your legitimate vendor already has your important information, so there is no need to verify it.

# CHAPTER TWELVE

# Will Retirement Drive You Crazy?

You spend years daydreaming of the day that you are free of the yoke of employment, but when it arrives it is not what you expected. Instead of just boredom, many retirees become depressed or, worse, seriously ill because of retirement. It is very important to replace your work activities with others such as travel, exercise, sports, community service, continuing education, and hobbies. According to Russ Wiles of the *Arizona Republic*, "Baby boomers will ride into retirement on motorbikes and in PT Cruisers, listening to classic rock and shot up with Botox. They say they want to retire earlier than their parents and lead active, independent lives filled with travel, volunteer work and perhaps an occasional trip to the plastic surgeon." "Boomers will look at retirement as more than just golf," said Bob Prisuta, director of research for AARP in Washington, DC. "Activities like skiing, swimming, running, and tennis will be more popular than they are now."

These great activities just do not happen; they need to be planned before you retire, just as you have planned for the financial aspects of retirement. David Bird, a partner in the financial planning firm of Strategic Planning Partners in Miami, suggests that your financial planning be married with your lifestyle planning so that there are no surprises and both can adjust accordingly to make both plans successful. He has been advising retirees for 24 years. One retiree in St. Petersburg, Florida, commented, "When I first retired, I tried fishing and playing tennis full time. These were the two leisure things I most wanted to do during my working career. As strange as it may sound, I found that if I went fishing or played tennis too many days, these leisure activities suddenly became work."

As Ronald Manheimer, the executive director of the North Carolina Center for Creative Retirement said, "We see people who've given all sorts of thought to the financial side of retirement, but they haven't dealt at all with the lifestyle part of the equation."

This need to plan is especially acute for men that have focused on work for most of their lives. Men are particularly susceptible to retirement blues if during their working life they did not allow for activities outside the job. Some males are forced to retire in corporate downsizings and they just stop being active and do not know what to do. Women on the other hand more often see the great possibilities for the new freedom from work that their husbands do not. Since women have more often juggled the competing roles of family caretaker, social secretary, community volunteer, and employee during their careers, women make the transition to retirement more easily and have no problem keeping active.

Psychologist Michael Longhurst of Australia explains there is a syndrome called the "honeymoon phase" during which many retirees view retirement very positively. It can last anywhere from a month to a year. The problem is that when this euphoria wears off retirees suddenly realize they are living out a fantasy and need more to sustain them in life. At the end of the honeymoon phase, retirees want structure, interests, creativity, mental stimulation, and a social network. Without structure "they become very anxious and depressed until they do something about it." A 9-to-5 job, although people hated it, pro-vided structure and stability that people depend on. That is why traditional unemployment is often very devastating emotion-ally. Self-esteem can plummet as well when retirees realize that they are dispensable and their employers manage to operate without them at work, and they no longer have the standing in the community that their jobs once conferred upon them. (See Jack Nicholson in the movie *About Schmidt* on this subject.) That is why it is very important that the newly retired plan to begin their retirement involves doing something interesting and productive.

"Find activities that are meaningful," wrote Walter Upde-grave in *Money* magazine's 2004 "Real World Retirement Guide." Nearly one quarter of adults age 65-plus participate in volunteer activities, almost half of them for religious-based groups. Is there a hobby that you wanted to pursue? A new ca-reer? A new skill that you want to develop? Instead of making the plans and feeling boxed in by your decision, "test spin" your retirement plans before you are retired and see if you re-ally like it. For example, if you think you want to become a chef because you enjoy cooking occasionally, take a short class or work in a restaurant kitchen locally before you enroll in a full-time cooking school in Italy. If you want to retire at the Outer Banks in North Carolina because you like to vacation there, stay there for more than a few weeks during several seasons of the year and see if you still like it.

If you are considering moving to the "ideal" retirement haven, consider the factors that a 2003 readers' survey of *Where to Retire* magazine considered the most important, in descending order:

1. Low crime rate
2. Active, clean, safe downtown
3. Good hospitals nearby

4. Low overall tax rate
5. Mild climate
6. Friendly, like-minded neighbors
7. Scenic beauty nearby
8. Low cost of living
9. Good recreational facilities
10. Low housing cost
11. Active social/cultural environment
12. Nearby airport with commercial service
13. Major city nearby
14. No state income tax
15. Continuing-care retirement communities nearby
16. Friends, relatives in area (surprising low on the list)
17. Full- or part-time employment opportunities
18. College town with adult education available

## STRESS AND RETIREMENT

Stress is unavoidable during your working career, but the "retirement blues" causes its own kind of stress. Intermittent stress is part of living—such as getting to the church on time—but if stress is prolonged, the hormones related to it can have serious effects on your memory, blood pressure, sleeping pattern, digestion, and immune system.

The National Mental Health Association has assembled a list of eight techniques to combat stress. If your stress is intense and unmanageable, they do recommend seeking professional help, but if it is the lower-level kind associated with retirement, review the following techniques:

1. Take one thing at time and be realistic. Take on your tasks in the order of importance. You have plenty of time; you're retired. Keeping lists helps to put things into per-

spective, keeps you organized, and provides a sense of accomplishment when you check them off as finished.

2. Do not be a superman or wonder woman. Don't take on more projects than you can handle. Don't be afraid to ask for help if you need it. Do not hesitate to say "NO." If you have too many things on your plate, say no. If you just don't want to do the activity, say no. Just because you are retired does not mean that you can't say no; your retirement time is your own. If you do not want to babysit the grandkids all the time, by all means say no.

3. Share your feelings. Seek support from your family and friends. Just venting helps. If you need help, ask.

4. Adjust expectations. Do not expect too much from yourself or from others. In retirement you do not need to keep up with the Joneses. Your retirement is your own. Do not exceed your planned budgets or push your physical limits trying to keep up with others.

5. Be flexible. Leave room for compromise in resolution of arguments, plans, and timetables.

6. Treat yourself. Retirement is for doing things that you enjoy.

7. Live healthy. Limit caffeine and alcohol, get enough sleep, exercise, and eat healthy foods. Your health will definitely affect your mood. If you are having persistent problems sleeping, check with your physician. Snoring might be the symptom of sleep apnea, a condition that can and should be treated.

8. Relax. Listening to music, exercising, practicing yoga, and meditating help you to live a less stressful life.

# RELATIONSHIPS

Marriages are particularly vulnerable in retirement. The first two years of retirement are like the first two years of marriage, a time to negotiate your roles and share your plans and dreams for the future. Jan Cullinane and Cathy Fitzgerald found in their research for *The New Retirement* that 60 percent of couples saw an improvement in their marriage during retirement. Without a job, the relationship is no longer "diluted by work any more." It is important to discuss and plan for your future *before* retirement. This may sound a lot like Dr. Phil—and I know that David Letterman makes fun of him—but planning is vitally important to enjoying your retirement years if you are married or living with a partner.

The "underfoot husbands" are those men who interfere with the duties their partners have successfully completed for years without them. Australian psychologist Michael Longhurst found that "the relationship can be affected by the husband following the wife around the house or going along to do the shopping and overriding his wife's decisions. It may sound silly but it came up time and time again." Other studies of couples in the United States mentioned the same thing as a prime cause of stress and arguments.

Longhurst found that couples involved in "purposeful" activities for at least five hours a week flourished. A purposeful activity is one that has a goal, or provides a service, such as volunteer work, a part-time job, higher education to attain a degree, or a craft or hobby. They suffered less from depression, anxiety, and stress than those who were not.

He also recommends building your own retirement structure by following routines and keeping to timetables. Exercise and proper diet also help to lower levels of anxiety. Exercise has been proven to help keep your brain fit as well.

The other critical asset Longhurst found for retiree couples was to have a support network to contact in times of crises and for recreation. Having a financial advisor to help sort through budgeting and income matters is also a plus. It helps to have these outsiders' opinions to diffuse arguments ("Retirement Blues," Pamela Wilson, *Daily Telegraph*, 7/31/00, p.82).

Alone time is critical to a healthy marriage. Syndicated columnist Janet Kidd Stewart stressed that couples need to jointly plan their retirement timing. If one working partner retires before the other, imbalances in the power in the relationship related to income arise. It is often good for the financial health of the family to have one spouse work to provide continuing health coverage for the couple. But couples need to deal with this situation and be honest about their own needs to each other. Stewart quoted a working wife saying, "We've always had a rhythm to our marriage. I was used to his being gone two to three nights a week and having my own time. Then when he retired, I put this expectation on myself that I needed to stay home, and I began to resent that. Finally one night I told him I was going out after work, and he said, 'Great!' "

Marriage is by no means magically more tranquil in retirement than while the partners were working. Some issues in a marriage that remain unresolved while working and look intractable will remain unresolved during retirement, such as how tidy the house should be. In a study of marriages over fourteen years at the University of Washington 69 percent of disagreements are never resolved. Virtually all couples, happy and unhappy, are going to argue. That is why couples need to understand that arguments will not stop, but because you have more time on your hands during retirement and more time together, couples need to fight more "effectively" to maintain their sanity and their marriages. The result has been a gradual shift to spouses' managing and accepting their discord, rather than trying to resolve the unresolvable. Howard Markman, co-director of the Center for Marital and Family Studies at the

University of Denver, said, "What tends to predict the future of a relationship is not what you argue about, but when you argue, and how you handle your negative emotions."

## The Eight Rules of Engagement

1. Choose the right time. Do not choose to argue while you are involved in other activities. Pick a time and a place. Some couples find it helpful to have a regular time to air grievances, which avoids eruptions and heated moments when tempers flair. With a time to argue set aside, the rest of the time you can relax.
2. Be focused on the disagreement, one thing at a time.
3. Don't generalize (as in "You always do X or Y").
4. Don't bring up past events and old grudges.
5. Don't interrupt; allow your spouse to make a point.
6. Don't use insults.
7. Don't use inflammatory language like "this marriage is doomed." Try to say "I" (as in "I think") rather than the more inflammatory "you" (as in "You don't").
8. After the argument, allow a bit of time to pass and have a "reconciliation conversation."

Source: Hillary Stout, "The Key to a Lasting Marriage: Combat," Wall Street Journal, 11/4/04, p. D1.

## DIVORCE AND RETIREMENT

Studies of couples who survive retirement and have made it to their 50th anniversaries have been conducted. In an article by Susan Reinhardt titled "Cooking up Lasting Marriages," she pinpoints trust, forgiveness, and commitment as the keys to stay together. "You choose to love just as you choose to forgive and stay with the one you're with." In addition, a sense of humor does not hurt.

For women, divorce during retirement can be devastating.

Often they have worked at jobs that do not provide a pension. Social Security benefits are also slashed as the separated spouse is not entitled to the full benefits of the ex-partner. And because retirement is later in life there is no real possibility to earn a full pension or substantial Social Security benefits on her own. Women are at a disadvantage to rebuild their financial security.

During a divorce, private pensions are not automatically divided. It must be spelled out in the divorce decree, in a document called a Qualified Domestic Relations Order (QUADRO). Without one a company has no power to allocate a pension to a former spouse. If the working spouse remarries, the new spouse would be entitled to any survivor benefits unless it is in writing otherwise. Social Security, on the other hand, has its own rules that apply to divorced spouses equally.

# CHAPTER THIRTEEN

# Really Running Out of Resources: What to Do

Sometimes unexpected circumstances can undo years of careful planning and savings. Bad investments or an extended illness can easily do it. Unfortunately, an extended stay in a nursing home or in a long-term care facility can drain your resources quicker than your portfolio can handle. Nursing-home costs can deplete a parent's life savings, and Baby Boomers are learning what comes next. This topic is as important for your future as for the future of your elderly parents. You may be financially secure, but if you support your parents or relatives you may be jeopardizing your own retirement. For instance, Nancy has planned well and saved for her own retirement. If she drains her nest egg to help support a friend or relative through a lengthy and costly disability, her own retirement may be put at risk.

Few people have costly long term care insurance and even for those who do, it is not enough to offset an indefinite draw on your resources. A nursing home can cost $5,000 a month. If you think you may need to live in a nursing home in the future because of deteriorating health, it is imperative that you plan ahead. If you are 65, Medicare can cover most of your costs; if not, you need to read further.

You can choose to deplete all your assets in a futile effort to pay your medical bills and ask for money from your family, or you can protect your assets. If you run out of assets to pay for the medical bills that exceed all your insurance coverages, Medicaid pays the rest of your bills, Medicare premiums, deductibles, co-payments, and even some services that Medicare does not. In 2001 Medicaid paid 47.5 percent of all nursing home costs. In addition Medicaid provides a $10 per month allowance for personal expenses. Medicaid is jointly funded from Federal and state sources, not from the Social Security Trust Fund.

You will have to tap your savings to get into the best nursing home. You must be able to pay the full charges for several months to qualify for admission. The facility wants to recover some of the revenues that will be lost when Medicaid begins payments. Assisted-living facilities are not covered by Medicaid, although some states are experimenting with a "Medicare waiver," which will provide a lower cost alternative to an expensive nursing home. In forty-nine states Medicaid pays for in-home care.

You qualify for Medicaid only when your assets have been exhausted. Your home will be sold when it is clear that you will not be returning. Generally, the state cannot touch money that you have given away three years or more before entering a nursing home facility. In some states your IRA assets are exempt from confiscation, but the minimum distributions must be turned over for your care.

Your spouse can keep the family home to live in and approximately $100,000 in assets. The exact figure depends on your state's rules. The spouse can also keep $1,500 to $2,500 of monthly income, but the excess must be turned over to the state. It is best to consult a lawyer experienced in Medicaid issues for advice about living trusts to protect your assets. If you have the benefit of knowing three years in advance that you'll need long-term care, you can "shift assets" to your family. An editorial, "Medicaid for Millionaires," in the *Wall Street Journal* on February 24, 2005, explained it:

> *"Since a home, business and a car of unlimited value are excluded from the calculation of assets, someone who wishes to qualify for Medicaid may shield his money by remodeling his house, investing in the family business, or purchasing expensive cars that he then gives away to family members (the notorious 'two Mercedes rule'). Term life insurance—also of unlimited value—is excluded as well.*

Consult your attorney to make sure it is done properly and legally.

As explained in the *Kiplinger's Personal Finance* magazine article by Kristen Davis, "When Mom's Money Runs Out," in November 2004, you need to do the following before you apply for Medicaid:

1. Apply for Medicaid before you run out of money, because Medicaid approval can take months for approval.
2. Consider setting up an irrevocable burial trust to fund a burial that you find appropriate. This trust will not be counted for your financial-eligibility test.
3. Pay off outstanding bills and debts before applying for Medicaid. Debts are not subtracted from your assets to determine your eligibility.
4. Prepare to present all your bank statements and financial records for three years (or five years if you have set up trusts).

You will probably need help in handling this matter because the rules are complicated. Whether you are making this decision for yourself or a family member, it is highly stressful. Seek out community resources to help:

The National Academy of Elder Care Law Attorneys (*www.naela.com*)
Eldercare Locator (*www.eldercare.gov*)
The National Association of Professional Geriatric Care Managers (*www.caremanger.org*)

## SUPPLEMENTAL SECURITY INCOME (SSI)

Supplemental Security Income (SSI) is another program for people with very few financial resources. It covers people who are age 65 or older, and blind or have a disability. Over 5 million people collect SSI. Although SSI is managed by the Social Security Administration, the Social Security Trust Fund does not pay for SSI. You apply for SSI through the regular SSA phone numbers and offices. Just like Medicaid, there are very stringent guidelines that govern this program. If you qualify you will receive a maximum of $579 per month for an individual and $869 for a couple (2005 figures). This amount is adjusted annually for inflation as measured by the CPI. There are also some regional cost-of-living adjustments.

From the maximum amount permitted, the SSA subtracts your income. It does not deduct the first $20 dollars of income a month from all sources. It does not count the first $65 a month of earned income and 50 percent of any earned income above $65. It does not count food stamps, shelter, or food assistance or most home energy assistance. For spousal benefits, a portion of the spouse's income is counted. If you had an income of, say, $1,100 and no other income at all, the entire $579 benefit would be wiped out. As you can see, this program is for the indigent poor.

In order to qualify for SSI or Medicaid your bank accounts and investments cannot be worth more than $2,000 for an individual or $3,000 for couples. Not counted in this total is your home, life insurance with a value of $1,500 or less, your car, burial plot, and $1,500 in a burial fund. Again, this program is only for the seniors with very limited resources.

If you qualify for SSI you probably qualify for Medicaid. Because of the stringent requirements and the thorough review of SSI applicants by the SSA, thirty-two states accept all the people on SSI for Medicaid without a separate application process. Seven states (AK, ID, KS, NE, NV, OR, UT) use the same rules for qualification, but require separate applications. In eleven states (CT, HI, IL, IN, MN, MO, ND, NH, OH, OK, VA) Medicaid has its own standards and separate applications.

## OTHER AVAILABLE SUPPORT

In addition to Medicaid and SSI, there are other resources available to seniors with few means. If you are living in your own home, you are probably eligible for property tax abatements. Local utilities provide heating and cooling assistance. Food stamps can stretch your food dollars. Meals on Wheels and other local charities can supply food.

For prescription drugs, many pharmaceutical companies have programs that deliver their drugs for free directly to those in true need. Check the information at *www.helpingpatients .org* or call 800-762-4636. There is also a program called the Medicine Program. For a small fee of $5 per drug, the program will help you apply for free drugs. Medicine Program's number is 866-694-3893. The new prescription drug benefits provided by Medicare are attractive, but they require a monthly premium and an annual deductible.

# CHAPTER FOURTEEN

# Do You Want to Take Action?
# Retirement Resources Guide

Throughout the book these are resources to help you answer your retirement questions. They are presented here for your convenience and a few others you will need.

## Social Security Information

**Requesting Your Benefits Statement**
Call 800-772-1213 or go to *www.ssa.gov*

**Estimating Your Benefits Yourself**
"Quick Calculator" on *www.ssa.gov*

**Applying for Benefits**
Call 800-772-1213 or go to *www.ssa.gov*

**Filing a Protective Application for Benefits by Mail**
Social Security Administration
Office of Central Operations
P.O. Box 17775
Baltimore, MD 21235-1213

### *Retirement Budgeting*
Vanguard Retirement Worksheet: *www.vanguard.com*

### Investment Resources

**Evaluating Your Portfolio**
Morningstar "Portfolio X-Ray" and Mutual Fund Evaluations:
*www.morningstar.com*

**Projecting Returns of Your Portfolio**
T. Rowe Price's Monte Carlo Portfolio Evaluator:
*www.troweprice.com*

**CDs and Mortgage Rate Shopping Guide**
*www.bankrate.com*

**Insurance Company Soundness Evaluator**
This is needed to evaluate the insurance companies that provide insurance and annuities that you may consider purchasing.
Ambest: *www.ambest.com*
Fitch: *www.fitchratings.com*
Moody's: *www.moodys.com*
Standard & Poor's: *www.standardpoor.com*

**Reverse Mortgages Information**
Government reverse mortgage information:
*www.hud.gov/offices/hsg/sfh/hecm/hecmlist.com* or
800-569-4287
Reverse mortgage calculator to see what you can borrow:
*www.aarp.org/revmort*
Help with getting a reverse mortgage: AARP Foundation
Network Counselors at *www.hecmresources.org/network.cfm*

## Getting Your Documents in Order

### Health Care Proxy

If you are unable to make medical decisions on your own, you must designate someone you trust who can. See *www .seniorsite.com,* "Proxy Form." Your physician and family should know whom you have appointed. Both the designated person and your doctor should have a copy of this form.

### Durable Power of Attorney

If you are incapacitated, this document allows someone to make financial and legal decisions for you. Go to *www.find legalforms.com* or *medlawplus.com.* These forms vary by state. Your relatives need to know whom you have named. That person should have a copy of the document.

### Living Will and Advance Directive

If you need extreme medical attention and cannot speak for yourself, what medical attention do you want to receive? This is a personal document and needs to be tailored for your needs and must comply with state law. Go to *www.legaldocs.com.* This document should also be shared with your doctor and family.

### Funeral Arrangements

Write a letter outlining what you want. For most of her life my mother said she wanted to be cremated. When she got older, she told my brother and me that she wanted a formal religious ceremony. If she hadn't told us, she would not have had the funeral she wanted because she died suddenly from pancreatic cancer.

### Will

Your will is a very important document. If you have a substantial or complicated estate, bickering relatives, and/or specific or unusual bequests, it is best to consult an attorney. Wills are governed by state law and need to be customized like medical directives to be less open to legal challenge. If you have a simple, straightforward situation, Quicken WillMaker Plus software is easy to use. It is updated each year and was judged number one by the *Wall Street Journal* and *USA Today*. There are free forms available on the web. If you have questions and consider estate planning important, do not rely on the free forms. Included in Quicken WillMaker Plus are the forms for living wills, health care directives, and durable power of attorney. A will may contain information that you do not want to share with your family while you are alive. Keep it with your attorney, the executor (if a different person), or with your personal papers. (Make sure your family knows their location.)

## Comments, suggestions?
## Contact your author, Steve Silbiger

*retire.early.question@juno.com*
*www.retire-early-question.com*

# INDEX